OAE 040 School Counselor

By: Preparing Teachers In America™

This page is intentionally left blank.

This publication is not an affiliation, or sponsorship, of Pearson Education or the National Evaluation Series.

© 2017 by Preparing Teachers In America

Publication by Preparing Teachers In America Publication Services, a division of Preparing Teachers In America

All rights reserved. The text of this publication, or any part thereof, may not be reproduced in any manner whatsoever without the written permission from Preparing Teachers In America. Any violation of copyright laws will be subject to possible criminal charges and/or civil penalties.

Printed in the United States of America

ISBN-13: 978-1540004062

ISBN-10: 1540004066

The author and the publisher make no warranties with respect to the correctness or completeness of the content contain in this publication and specifically disclaim all warranties whatsoever. Advice, strategies, and suggestions described may not be suitable for every case. Providing web addresses or other (information) services in this publication does not mean/imply that the author or publisher endorses information or websites. Neither the author nor publisher shall be liable for damages arising herefrom. Websites may be infected by computer viruses. The author and publisher shall not be held responsible for any damage resulted herefrom. Websites (content) may have altered since the time the author described them in this booklet and this booklet is read. There are no guarantees attached to the publication. The content of this publication is best practices, suggestions, common mistakes, and interpretation, and the author and the publisher are not responsible for any information contained in the publication.

Any services provided by the publication, authors, or company are with the understanding that services can be terminated with or without notice. In rendering services, the author and the publisher are not responsible for any information communicated. Users agree not to hold the service (author/publisher/company) or its employees liable for any services (information) provided or any information displayed on the website. Users release the service from any claims or any kind of damage. The author, publisher, services, and/or company are not responsible for any accuracy or legitimacy of the information provided during rendering services. There are no guarantees attached to services.

No institutions (public or private) have permission to reproduce (in any form) the contents of this publication.

This page is intentionally left blank.

Free Online Email Tutoring Services

All preparation guides purchased directly from Preparing Teachers In America includes a free three month email tutoring subscription. Any resale of preparation guides does not qualify for a free email tutoring subscription.

What is Email Tutoring?

Email Tutoring allows buyers to send questions to tutors via email. Buyers can send any questions regarding the exam processes, strategies, content questions, or practice questions.

Preparing Teachers In America reserves the right not to answer questions with or without reason(s).

How to use Email Tutoring?

Buyers need to send an email to onlinepreparationservices@gmail.com requesting email tutoring services. Buyers may be required to confirm the email address used to purchase the preparation guide or additional information prior to using email tutoring. Once email tutoring subscription is confirmed, buyers will be provided an email address to send questions to. The three month period will start the day the subscription is confirmed.

Any misuse of email tutoring services will result in termination of service. Preparing Teachers In America reserves the right to terminate email tutoring subscription at anytime with or without notice.

Comments and Suggestions

All comments and suggestions for improvements for the study guide and email tutoring services need to be sent to onlinepreparationservices@gmail.com.

This page is intentionally left blank.

Table of Content

About the Exam and Study Guide 1

School Counselor Exam Answer Sheet 5

Practice Exam Questions – School Counselor 7

School Counselor Exam - Correct Answer Sheet 67

Practice Exam Questions and Explanation – School Counselor 69

This page is intentionally left blank.

About the Exam and Study Guide

What is the OAE School Counselor Exam?

The OAE School Counselor is an exam to test potential individuals' competencies in counseling skills necessary to pursue a school counselor role in institutions. The exam is aligned with the updated practices used to ensure effective counseling, and the exam covers the following content areas:

- School Development and Learning
- Comprehensive School Counseling Program
- Professional Knowledge and Practice

The exam is timed at 180 minutes and consists of 150 select response questions. The exam questions are based on knowledge obtained in school counseling programs. The exam contains some questions that may not count toward the score.

What topics are covered on the exam?

The following are some topics covered on the exam:

- human development from early childhood to young adulthood
- learning process and factors that affect learning
- development and implementation of a guidance curriculum
- individual planning to help students establish goals
- providing responsive services to meet students' needs
- principles of leadership to support the educational system
- applications of testing and assessment
- strategies for developing effective relationships
- understand roles, responsibilities, and professional standards of school counselors
- knowledge of various theories of development
- knowledge of diagnostic and remediation activities
- knowledge of crisis counseling methods

What is included in this study guide book?

This guide includes one full length practice exams for the School Counselor Exam along with detail explanations. The recommendation is to take the exams under exam conditions and a quiet environment.

This page is intentionally left blank.

Practice Test 1

This page is intentionally left blank.

School Counselor Exam Answer Sheet

Below is an optional answer sheet to use to document answers.

Question Number	Selected Answer	Question Number	Selected Answer	Question Number	Selected Answer	Question Number	Selected Answer	Question Number	Selected Answer
1		31		61		91		121	
2		32		62		92		122	
3		33		63		93		123	
4		34		64		94		124	
5		35		65		95		125	
6		36		66		96		126	
7		37		67		97		127	
8		38		68		98		128	
9		39		69		99		129	
10		40		70		100		130	
11		41		71		101		131	
12		42		72		102		132	
13		43		73		103		133	
14		44		74		104		134	
15		45		75		105		135	
16		46		76		106		136	
17		47		77		107		137	
18		48		78		108		138	
19		49		79		109		139	
20		50		80		110		140	
21		51		81		111		141	
22		52		82		112		142	
23		53		83		113		143	
24		54		84		114		144	
25		55		85		115		145	
26		56		86		116		146	
27		57		87		117		147	
28		58		88		118		148	
29		59		89		119		149	
30		60		90		120		150	

This page is intentionally left blank.

Practice Exam Questions – School Counselor

QUESTION 1

A student's father called the school counselor and told the counselor that his son had shared with him that one of his friends was being physically abused. The school counselor met with the boy in question; however, he denied being abused. As a school counselor, which of the following is the best action to pursue further?

- A. do nothing as the boy denied the physical abuse
- B. continue to investigate to confirm if abuse occurred
- C. report the suspected child abuse per state law
- D. involve the school principal to discuss with the boy

Answer:

QUESTION 2

A student has informed the school counselor that she thinks she is pregnant and plans to get an abortion without telling her parents. Which of the following is the first question that the school counselor should inquire?

- A. Was the sex consensual?
- B. How old is the father of the baby?
- C. Did you confirm that you are pregnant?
- D. How is your relationship with your parent?

Answer:

QUESTION 3

A student has recently told the school counselor that she cuts herself. The cuts shown do not indicate that the student is suicidal. Which of the following is the best first action to take in this situation?

- A. contact child protective services
- B. contact the parents to help solve the problem
- C. understand the reasoning for the cutting behavior
- D. enroll the student in therapy sessions with the school psychologist

Answer:

QUESTION 4

Which of the following court cases consistently found that school counselors did not "owe a legal duty" to prevent a student's suicide?

- A. Eisel vs. Montgomery County Board of Education of 1991
- B. James vs. American School Counselor Association of 2001
- C. Eisel vs. American School Counselor Association of 2001
- D. James vs. Montgomery County Board of Education of 1991

Answer:

QUESTION 5

A student has threatened suicide and likely going to commit suicide. The school counselors' legal liability ends when

- A. the student gets help.
- B. the counselor recommends appropriate action to teachers.
- C. the counselor recommends appropriate action to school officials.
- D. the student is put on suicide watch.

Answer:

QUESTION 6

Jenny is the school counselor at a small high school. Her daughter is planning to attend the same school next year. If the daughter has personal issues to discuss, as the school counselor, Jenny's best action is to:

- A. provide school counseling services to her daughter
- B. provide parenting advice to her daughter
- C. seek outside consultation for her daughter
- D. request principal to support her daughter

Answer:

QUESTION 7

Which of the following best describes appropriate note taking for school counselors?

- A. minimal notes, containing student name, time and a few details as a memory aid
- B. minimal notes, containing student name, time and a many details
- C. notes containing student name, problem, and treatment plan
- D. minimal notes, containing student name, time and a treatment plan

Answer:

QUESTION 8

Family Education Rights and Privacy Act (FERPA) gives parents the right to see all of the following except

- A. standardize test scores.
- B. report card grades.
- C. notes taken by school counselors.
- D. all of the above.

Answer:

QUESTION 9

A school is planning to have a group of students complete multiple assessments to determine if they are classified as gifted and talented. In respect to the data obtained from the assessment, the school counselor's role is to

- A. analyze data.
- B. administer test.
- C. collect data.
- D. coordinate test.

Answer:

QUESTION 10

A school counselor is helping all students by getting them to:

- develop a portfolio to show strengths and interests
- apply strategies to accomplish future academic and career success
- show the connection between coursework and life experiences

These actions best describe the school counselor helping students

A. get ready for college.
B. get ready to go to high school.
C. get ready to help student decide on a career.
D. get ready for senior year of high school education.

Answer:

QUESTION 11

Which of the following is critical to ensure a positive effect the school counselor and the school counseling program have on students and school stakeholders?

A. school counselor performance evaluation
B. confidentiality
C. annual school goals
D. high scores on standardize tests

Answer:

QUESTION 12

In regards to bullying, the school counselor's role include all the following except?

A. collaborating with others to promote safe schools and confront issues
B. encourage the development of policies supporting a safe school environment
C. punish students who are engaging in bullying acts
D. provide leadership in implementing school-wide prevention programs

Answer:

QUESTION 13

_____ is when schools along with social institutions and parents support the positive character development of children and adults.

A. Development
B. Character education
C. School counseling program
D. Positive relationship

Answer:

QUESTION 14

I. increased risk of child abuse
II. erosion of trust between an adult and child
III. adverse effects on cognitive development

All of the above best describe negative effects of which of the following?

A. Family problems
B. Corporal punishment
C. Drinking
D. Neglect

Answer:

QUESTION 15

Using behavioral contracts, setting realistic expectations, enforcing rules consistently, and emphasizing positive behaviors of students are alternatives to which of the following?

- A. suspending
- B. retaining
- C. expelling
- D. whipping

Answer:

QUESTION 16

Which of the following is a way for a school counselor to foster increased awareness, understanding and appreciation of cultural diversity in the school?

- A. teach tolerance
- B. address issues of nonviolence
- C. discuss social justice
- D. all of the above

Answer:

QUESTION 17

Disruptive student behavior is one of the most significant, ongoing problems confronting schools. To establish and maintain safe and respectful learning environments, school counselors must ensure

- A. effective discipline programs.
- B. rules are being clearly communicated.
- C. constructed feedback to students
- D. teachers are trained to handle disruptive behavior

Answer:

QUESTION 18

A school counselor must recognize that _____ have encountered barriers to participating in a rigorous curriculum and higher level classes.

A. African Americans
B. underrepresented populations
C. young children
D. special education students with severe disability

Answer:

QUESTION 19

Which of the following is not within the scope of a school counselor's responsibility?

A. individual counseling
B. group counseling
C. therapy addressing psychological disorders
D. respond to student mental health crises

Answer:

QUESTION 20

Which of the following is not appropriate for a school counselor to undertake when working with a LGBTQ (lesbian, gay, bisexual, transgender and questioning) student?

A. promote academic achievement
B. encourage the student to select a certain identity
C. counsel students with feelings about their sexual orientation
D. encourage the student not to be violent when confronted with bullying

Answer:

QUESTION 21

    I.   parents
    II. teachers
    III. students

School counselors are skilled in both educating and counseling, allowing them to function as a facilitator among which of the following from above?

A. I and II
B. I and III
C. II and III
D. I, II, and III

Answer:

QUESTION 22

Which of the following best completes the statement below?

School counselors provide services to _____.

A. all students
B. students in need
C. all school members
D. students and family members

Answer:

QUESTION 23

All of the following are types of behavior therapy interventions except:

A. systematic desensitization
B. flooding
C. aversion conditioning
D. therapeutic transference

Answer:

QUESTION 24

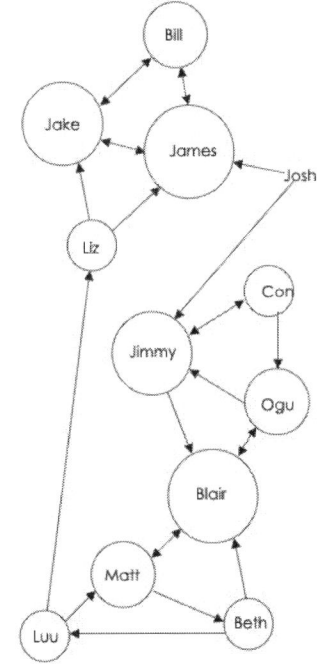

A school counselor could best use the sociogram shown above to assess which of the following elements of sixth-grade students' social development?

A. popularity
B. peer acceptance
C. development
D. communication skills

Answer:

QUESTION 25

Matt is a 10-year-old Caucasian male. He was referred to the school counselor, Ms. Blake, by Ms. James, his 4th-grade teacher, who has noticed ongoing behavioral problems in class. Matt is unable to focus, does not listen, and has difficulty communicating with classmates. Ms. Blake has observed the student on the playground having difficulty interacting with his peers. As the school counselor, Ms. Blake next best option is which of the following?

A. recommend to visit a doctor to see if he has Attention Deficit Hyperactivity Disorder
B. contact the parent to understand the behavior displayed outside of school
C. have the student participate in weekly discussion with the school counselor
D. recommend the student be placed in special education classes

Answer:

QUESTION 26

A school counselor has observed a student constantly describing objects such as buses and chairs as having feelings and other lifelike properties. Which of the following of Jean Piaget's concepts is best shown by this behavior?

A. artificialism
B. animism
C. conservation
D. equilibrium

Answer:

QUESTION 27

During a classroom guidance lesson, an elementary school counselor assists a student by focusing on tasks that a child can perform with the help and guidance of others but cannot yet perform independently. Providing such assistance is best related to which of Lev Vygotsky's concept?

   A. scaffolding
   B. differentiation
   C. intersubjectivity
   D. zone of proximal development

Answer:

QUESTION 28

Which of the following is considered an external referral in regards to school counseling services?

   A. teachers
   B. nurses
   C. peers
   D. parents

Answer:

QUESTION 29

Several first grade teachers approached the school counselor with concerns that their students are having behavior issues. Issues include refusing to share, pushing each other, and calling each other names. To support the teachers, the school counselor plans to implement classroom guidance lessons focused on teaching social skills to all first grade students. Of the following, which is the best way for the teacher to develop appropriate curriculum for the first grade students?

   A. Search the Internet for lesson plans developed by other counselors.
   B. Ask teachers to develop the lesson plan and make necessary changes.
   C. Review professional materials and ASCA website.
   D. Use previous year lessons related to anger management.

Answer:

QUESTION 30

Several first grade teachers approached the school counselor with concerns that their students are having behavior issues. Issues include refusing to share, pushing each other, and calling each other names. To support the teachers, the school counselor plans to implement classroom guidance lessons focused on teaching social skills to all first grade students. After delivering the lesson to the first grade students, which of the following is the best secondary intervention approach?

- A. individual coaching
- B. small-group counseling
- C. student-parent counseling
- D. psychoeducational group counseling

Answer:

QUESTION 31

A student has approached the school counselor for a letter of recommendation for a college application. The counselor has agreed to provide a letter of recommendation, in which the counselor writes about the student's good academic standing, honest behavior, and commitment to succeed. Several weeks later, the counselor finds out that the student has fabricated some parts of the personal essay for the college application. The school counselor is obligated to

- A. do nothing in this situation.
- B. retract the letter of recommendation.
- C. require the student to re-submit the personal essay.
- D. inform the college of the fabricated parts of the personal essay.

Answer:

QUESTION 32

John, a ninth-grade student, has committed suicide on school property. As the school counselor, which of the following is not an action to take during the first few days of this tragic event?

    A. provide moral support to the students
    B. engage with parents on supporting students
    C. conduct group counseling with students close to John
    D. investigate the reasons for the student committing suicide

Answer:

QUESTION 33

    I. strong reading skills and large vocabulary
    II. strong motivation to be focused in particular area
    III. strong communication skills with peers

Of the above, which of the following are clear indication(s) of a gifted child?

    A. I only
    B. I and II
    C. I and III
    D. I, II, and III

Answer:

QUESTION 34

_____ is an effective and efficient way to deliver direct services to students in which a counselor works with multiple students simultaneously to address common concerns or problem behavior.

    A. School counseling curriculum
    B. Therapy counseling
    C. Group counseling
    D. Pair counseling

Answer:

QUESTION 35

A school counselor has been working with a student for several months regarding communication and behavioral issues. The counselor has not seen any progress since she started working with the student. Which of the following is the best approach to take next?

- A. send the student to the school psychologist
- B. have the student work with external counselor
- C. have the student work with another internal counselor
- D. have the student work with the special education department

Answer:

QUESTION 36

Which of the following is not a post-action after a serious crisis has occurred on school property?

- A. Reassure individuals that the world is a good place, however that there are people who do bad things.
- B. Keep all information from the kids to prevent them from becoming scared.
- C. Ensure attachments and relationships.
- D. Listen to individuals' fears and concerns.

Answer:

QUESTION 37

Which of the following is not an external consultee?

- A. tutors
- B. parents
- C. school nurse
- D. agency personal

Answer:

QUESTION 38

The ASCA National Model: A Framework for School Counseling Programs addresses which of the three domains?

- A. individual, small-group, and large-group classroom guidance
- B. communication, communities, and collaboration
- C. career, academic, and personal-social development
- D. foundations, accountability, and management

Answer:

QUESTION 39

A ninth-grade student is going through a period of mild to moderate depression, in which the student is having negative views of self, the world in general, and the future. Which of the following is the best first approach for the school counselor to take?

- A. cognitive therapeutic approach
- B. refer to medical professional
- C. open-ended communication approach
- D. provide anxiety medication

Answer:

QUESTION 40

Which of the following is NOT one of the major components of the ASCA National Model?

- A. foundation
- B. management
- C. performance
- D. accountability

Answer:

QUESTION 41

A middle school class is going on a field trip to the history museum. Information has surfaced that the bus has been in an accident in which three students are injured. As a member of the school's emergency response team, which of the following steps should the school counselor take first?

A. confirm that the information surfacing is accurate
B. ensure that the police and ambulances are on the location of the accident
C. call the parents of all students to provide update on condition
D. provide support to the students and teachers impacted by the accident

Answer:

QUESTION 42

I. keeping clerical records
II. interpreting student records
III. computing grade-point averages

Of the above, which of the following is/are inappropriate for school counselors to undertake?

A. I only
B. I and II
C. I and III
D. I, II, and III

Answer:

QUESTION 43

Which of the following is the first stage in Erik Erikson's theory of personality development?

A. autonomy vs. shame
B. intimacy vs. inferiority
C. trust vs. mistrust
D. ego integrity vs. despair

Answer:

QUESTION 44

    I.   providing planning career advice

    II.   supporting poor performing students

    III.   giving substance abuse education

The above best describes a school counselor providing support to which of the following group of students?

- A. early childhood
- B. middle school
- C. elementary
- D. high school

Answer:

QUESTION 45

A high school counselor is seeking to implement technology in helping place students in their desired elective classes. Which of the following types of software would be the best to use?

- A. database
- B. word processing
- C. excel document
- D. adobe editor

Answer:

QUESTION 46

A school counselor takes notes of discussion with students on a notepad. Ethical standards require that the counselor

- A. transfer the notes to a computer.
- B. memorize the notes and destroy the notes immediately.
- C. make a back up copy of the notes in case there are lost.
- D. establish a time limit for properly purging students' files.

Answer:

QUESTION 47

Which of the following situations will require the school counselor to provide the longest duration support?

- A. a fifth-grader who lost her father in a car accident
- B. a teacher who lost her husband in a car accident
- C. writing a student a letter of recommendation for a scholarship program
- D. a student transitioning from special education class to general education class

Answer:

QUESTION 48

Which of the following provides protection to school counselors in case of any malpractice situations?

- A. lobbying efforts
- B. counselor union
- C. liability insurance
- D. professional development

Answer:

QUESTION 49

A student has come to the school counselor to talk about issues she is having since her father moved to another city and left her mother. It would likely be most critical to the student for the school counselor to

- A. keep conversation confidential.
- B. provide positive feedback.
- C. show respect for the family structure.
- D. provide hope for her father to return.

Answer:

QUESTION 50

A school counselor is assisting a second grader deal with the death of her mother. As a school counselor, it is extremely critical to

- A. give the student the vocabulary to express her feelings
- B. provide the student with personal time during school time
- C. give examples of how the student should feel
- D. ensure the student this feeling is temporary

Answer:

QUESTION 51

- I. increase job satisfaction
- II. better manage time
- III. increase productivity

Of the above, which of the following is/are reason for ensuring organization in school counseling programs?

- A. I only
- B. I and II
- C. II and III
- D. I, II, and III

Answer:

QUESTION 52

    I.   analyzing disaggregated data

    II.   assisting with duties in the principal's office

    III.   coordinating achievement testing programs

Of the above, which of the following is/are appropriate behavior(s) for school counselors?

    A. I only
    B. I and II
    C. I and III
    D. I, II, and III

Answer:

QUESTION 53

A school counselor is analyzing participation rates in Gifted and Talented courses by gender and determines that males are heavily represented in Math and Science courses but poorly represented in English. Which of the following is the most appropriate action for the counselor to undertake?

    A. balance the enrollment of males and females in Gifted and Talented courses
    B. review the procedures related to referring students to Gifted and Talented courses
    C. seek students who are interested in Gifted and Talented courses to balance the enrollment data
    D. share concerns with the principal to formally open an inquiry into Gifted and Talented enrollment process

Answer:

QUESTION 54

A new school counselor has been hired at the local middle school. The school counselor comes from a wealthy family and previously worked in a private school. The middle school is located in a poor area, where annual income per family is less than $30,000. The crime rate in the location is higher than other surrounding areas. Which of the following is the best for the school counselor to undertake to better understand the environment the students are coming from?

A. do online research on the community
B. talk to students about life outside of school
C. tour the streets and community
D. attend open house at the school

Answer:

QUESTION 55

Teachers are allowed to have emergency license to continue teaching temporary if they do not have all their certification exam passed; this is not the case for school counselors. Which of the following best explain the reason for this difference in expectations for teachers and school counselors when it comes to certification exams?

A. there are few school counselors than teachers
B. there is a higher demand for teachers
C. school counselors deal with more sensitive matters
D. school counselors exams are a lot easier than teachers exams

Answer:

QUESTION 56

Which of the following is the best way for a school counselor to promote holistic student development?

    A. require teachers to have lessons geared toward holistic student development
    B. apply current research regarding nutrition and family systems
    C. have students fill survey on questions related to their home development
    D. give students the opportunity to express themselves

Answer:

QUESTION 57

Which of the following is the best way for a school counselor to distribute information on scholarships and colleges for all students?

    A. email the information to all students
    B. place the information on bulletin near the cafeteria
    C. send the information to English teachers to distribute to students
    D. have a webpage on the school website related to college readiness

Answer:

QUESTION 58

Which of the following is likely the best topic that a school counselor can teach in a regular elementary school classroom setting?

    A. sex education
    B. anger management skills
    C. scientific inquiry process
    D. abortion

Answer:

QUESTION 59

I. addresses the immediate concerns of all students
II. prevention and intervention
III. school counselor role includes consulting and referring

The above describes which of the following Components of a Comprehensive School Counseling Program?

A. Guidance Curriculum
B. Individual Planning
C. Responsive Services
D. Monitoring Progress

Answer:

QUESTION 60

A middle school counselor receives a call from the father of a student the counselor is supporting. The student has been unwilling in participating in school activities. The student has been talking to the counselor about his shyness, anxiety around peers, and negative self-concept. The father is aware of his son seeking support from the school counselor, and the father thanks the counselor for talking to his son. In addition, the father asks what his son has been talking about in the counseling sessions, and asks as to whether there is any way in which he can be supportive. Which of the following is the best action to take for the school counselor?

A. inform the father of the sessions and provide suggestion to what to do at home
B. inform in general terms what parents can do to be supportive without communicating details of the student's conversation
C. inform the father that he is not allowed to ask for information about what his son informed the school counselor
D. inform the father on the confidential nature of the counseling relationship between the counselor and student

Answer:

QUESTION 61

A first year reading teacher comes to the school counselor in misery because of the behavior of an extremely hyperactive student in her classroom. She has tried multiple strategies to get the student to behave appropriately, but she is not at her whit's end. She has not contacted the parents yet and the student has now been tested for ADHD. As a school counselor, which of the following is NOT the action to take in this situation?

A. suggest the teacher provide more attention to the student during instruction
B. integrate technology to calm the student down
C. suggest that he be tested for ADHD
D. suggest to provide incentives (ex. extra breaks) when working through lengthy tasks or activities

Answer:

QUESTION 62

There are three school counselors at a high school that supports nearly 500 students. One of the school counselors has decided to take maternity leave. Soon after, another school counselor resigned. The remaining school counselor is stomped with work as she is now nearly supporting 500 students. Which of the following is the best approach for the school counselor to do during this situation to best support the school?

A. hire an administrative assistant that can support some minor issues
B. focus on major issues that surface
C. push some students to the assistant principal
D. do not focus on the other two counselors workload

Answer:

QUESTION 63

When establishing school counseling programs, which of the following is the most critical to consider for the school counselor?

- A. ensuring that the program has a long term vision
- B. identifying program belief that address how all students benefit
- C. ensuring that resources are available to provide appropriate support
- D. getting all staff, parents, and students aligned to the school counseling programs

Answer:

QUESTION 64

Which of the following stages defines sexual maturity based on Sigmund Freud's theory of psychosexual development?

- A. phallic
- B. genital
- C. anal
- D. latency

Answer:

QUESTION 65

In which of the following situation is a certified counselor not required in school institutions?

- A. a school with little population
- B. an early childhood school
- C. a newly built public school
- D. a private school

Answer:

QUESTION 66

    I.   cognitive

    II.   behavior

    III. affective

Of the above, which of the following do school counselors have impact on?

A. I only
B. I and II
C. II and III
D. I, II, and III

Answer:

QUESTION 67

A school counselor notices that a student's math standardize test scores are nearly perfect for several consecutive years. However, classroom grades on assignments and report card are below average or at average. Which of the following is the best first step to take to better understand the reasoning for the gap?

A. talk to the math teacher to get the math teacher's perspective on the gap
B. observe how the math teacher is providing instruction to the student
C. question the student regarding the gap and how the counselor can help
D. confirm that the student is not cheating on standardize tests

Answer:

QUESTION 68

Which of the following is NOT considered a self-management skill?

- A. demonstrate ability to overcome barriers to learning
- B. demonstrate perseverance to achieve long- and short-term goals
- C. demonstrate critical-thinking skills to make informed decisions
- D. demonstrate ability to assume responsibility

Answer:

QUESTION 69

In a session with a school counselor, a student provides very slight indication that the student might be having an inappropriate relationship with a teacher. What is the best action for the school counselor to take?

- A. move to another topic
- B. ignore the comment by the student
- C. ask more questions to get better understanding
- D. report the conversation to the school principal

Answer:

QUESTION 70

Steps to Program Development

1.	Planning
2.	Building the Foundation
3.	Designing the Delivery System
4.	Setting up the School Counseling Program
5.	Working the School Counseling Program
6.	Promoting the School Counseling Program
7.	?

Which of the follow completes the table above regarding steps to developing school counseling program?

A. Engaging teachers in participating
B. Monitoring program results
C. Ensuring all students benefit
D. Delivering the program

Answer:

QUESTION 71

Which of the following is the best for a school counselor to do to support English teachers in developing a lesson that delivers the guidance curriculum related to peer pressure?

A. develop a slide pack on key aspects of peer pressure and the objectives of the guidance curriculum related to peer pressure
B. conduct a training session with all teachers on peer pressure
C. give teachers videos related to peer pressuring to use during the lesson
D. provide assessment tools on guidance curriculum related to peer pressure to ensure students' learning

Answer:

QUESTION 72

A student has informed the school counselor that he will not be applying to colleges as his father got deported. The student does not see a point in getting further education as he will have to support his family. What can the school counselor do to assist the student?

  A. talk to the student about work and school life balance
  B. get the student connected with a immigration attorney
  C. discuss the long term benefits of a college education for his family
  D. talk about financial aid options available

Answer:

QUESTION 73

A school counselor is providing students support in career exploration, and teaching respect for self and others. Which grade level is the school counselor supporting?

  A. second grade
  B. fifth grade
  C. seventh grade
  D. eleventh grade

Answer:

QUESTION 74

Which of the following best describes situation where school counselor can break confidentiality?

  A. a student has cheated on homework assignment
  B. other students are at harm
  C. refusing to comply to punishment
  D. student is thinking about running away

Answer:

QUESTION 75

According to John Holland's Theory of Vocational, which term describes students who are thinking rather than acting, and organizing and understanding rather than dominating or persuading?

- A. realistic
- B. social
- C. investigative
- D. enterprising

Answer:

QUESTION 76

Juan, a 19-year old high school senior, tells the school counselor that he plans to marry his 18-year-old girlfriend after graduation. Legally, the school counselor is required to

- A. call the parents of both students to inform them of the situation.
- B. inform the students they can't get married.
- C. do nothing since the students are of legal age to get married.
- D. do an exploration session with the two students to determine if marrying is the best option.

Answer:

QUESTION 77

Below is a document that the school counselor uses to gather information about students to better support them.

Student Behavior Data Collection Form

STUDENT_____ TEACHER_____ DATE_____

Performance Indicators: (+)=Excellent, (I)=Satisfactory, (-)=Area of Concern

Teacher Concerns (mark with X)	Observed Behaviors	Marking Period 1	Marking Period 2	Marking Period 3	Marking Period 4	Marking Period 5
	Section 1: Personal Development					
	Cooperates with others					
	Shows respect for others					
	Allows others to work undisturbed					
	Accepts responsibility for own misbehavior (e.g., provoking fights, bullying, fighting, defiant, anger, stealing)					
	Emotional Issues (e.g., perfectionism, anxiety anger, depression, suicide, aggression, withdrawn, low self-esteem)					
	Section 2: Career Development					
	Awareness of the World of Work					
	Self-Appraisal					
	Decision Making					
	Goal Setting					
	Section 3: Add Other Concerns:					
	External Issues (e.g., divorce, death, abuse, socio-economic, incarceration, military deployment)					
	Other					
	Section 4: School Record Data					
	Attendance: # of days absent					
	Attendance: # of days tardy					
	Discipline: # of referrals					
	Grades					
	School nurse visits					
	Test Scores					

In the above Student Behavior Data Collection Form, which of the following mistakes must be corrected?

A. Change performance indicators to a number system instead of excellent, satisfactory, and area of concern.
B. Teacher Rating needs to be changed to School Counselor Rating.
C. Remove the Marking Period 5 as four periods is sufficient.
D. Remove teacher concern column.

Answer:

QUESTION 78

In the observed behavior column, which of the following sections needs to be included to get a full picture of the students?

A. Family Development
B. Academic Development
C. Social Development
D. Peer Interaction

Answer:

QUESTION 79

I. flexibility
II. willingness to listen
III. empathy

School counselors are advocates. Of the above, which of the following are characteristics that describe being an advocate?

A. I only
B. I and II
C. II and III
D. I, II, and III

Answer:

QUESTION 80

A school counselor is supporting a student that is feeling inferior. The school counselor encourages the student to be well aware of her surrounding and environment. As time goes by, the student learns to grapple her conscious levels of thought and is responsible for taking charge of changing behaviors. This situation best showed which of the following counseling theories?

A. The Gestalt Approach
B. The Person-Centered Approach
C. The Individual Psychology Approach
D. The Behavioral Approach

Answer:

QUESTION 81

A recent school survey showed that ninth grade female students are not interested in math and science subjects. In addition, recent assessment shows that male students are doing a lot better in math and science courses. The school counselor is looking to encourage more female students to become interested in math and science. Which of the following would be the best strategy to achieve this goal?

A. assign math and science electives for female students
B. start tutoring and mentoring program to increase female confidence in math and science
C. have a group session with females to understand why they don't like math and science subjects
D. encourage female students who are performing well to take more math and science courses

Answer:

QUESTION 82

    I.   facilitate the development of a plan of action

    II.   encourage the student to be more independent

    III.   be accessible to facilitate understanding between all involved parties (family, student, the future place of higher education).

Jimmy is starting his senior year at Roger High School. Since elementary school, he has had an IEP. As he has progressed in the educational system, his needs have changed as well. Jimmy is more concerned about his disability as he prepares for college. He and his parents have scheduled an appointment to speak with the school counselor. Of the above, which of the following is/are appropriate for the school counselor?

    A. II only
    B. III only
    C. I and III
    D. I, II and III

Answer:

QUESTION 83

Which of the following is an indirect measure of achievement?

    A. test results
    B. retention rates
    C. gifted screening
    D. rank in class

Answer:

QUESTION 84

Which of the following situations is best for the school counselor to use solution focused counseling?

- A. an elementary student bullying classmates
- B. a student worried about what career path to take
- C. a student missing class three days of the week
- D. a student with ADHD who is unwilling to complete assignments

Answer:

QUESTION 85

A high school counselor is working with a local college on implementing character education program. The local college professor has asked the school counselor to participate in a study to assess the impact of the character education classroom guidance program on the behavior of 10 children. For the study, the disciplinary records of these students will be used to complete the data. The school counselor has agreed to participate. Why is the school counselor agreeing to participate concerning?

- A. the counselor did not ask the principal for permission
- B. the counselor did not ask the parents for permission
- C. the counselor might be violating FERPA laws
- D. the counselor did nothing that is concerning

Answer:

QUESTION 86

   I. clarify ground rules and guidelines
   II. discuss how to take notes
   III. discuss confidentiality
   IV. discuss active listening for each other

To ensure effective group counseling, in the first session, the high school counselor must discuss which of the following from above?

   A. I and II
   B. II and III
   C. I, III, and IV
   D. I, II, III, and IV

Answer:

QUESTION 87

A school counselor can provide professional counseling services to students referred by:

   A. teachers
   B. peers
   C. nurse
   D. all of the above

Answer:

QUESTION 88

The Accountability Process

Step	Description
1	Mission - Connect the design and implementation of the school counseling program to the mission of the school.
2	Elements - Identify and examine the critical elements of the available data that are important to the school's mission.
3	Analyze - Analyze the critical data elements to see what they reveal, to identify problem areas, to establish baselines, and to set objectives.
4	Stakeholders-Unite – Identify stakeholders to be involved in addressing the movement of the critical data elements.
5	?
6	Educate – Inform all stakeholders of the changes in the targeted data elements that show the positive impact the school counseling program is having on student success.

Which of the following is the best description for Step 5?

A. Review – Reanalyze to determine whether the targeted results were satisfied.
B. Confirm – Rerun the program analysis to ensure the results are accurate.
C. Results – Reanalyze to determine whether the targeted results were satisfied.
D. Replicate – Rerun the program analysis to ensure the results are accurate.

Answer:

QUESTION 89

Which of the following is NOT one of the major components of a comprehensive counseling and guidance program?

- A. Guidance Curriculum
- B. Individual Planning
- C. Responsive Services
- D. Monitoring Progress

Answer:

QUESTION 90

Which of the following best describes how might a student's test score be affected by a recent death in the family?

- A. remain the same
- B. marginally increase
- C. decrease substantially
- D. reduce to average scores

Answer:

QUESTION 91

According to Erik Erikson's theory of human development, individuals gain a sense of competency and accomplishment between the ages of _____.

- A. 3 and 5
- B. 6 and 12
- C. 13 and 15
- D. 15 and 18

Answer:

QUESTION 92

_____ give empirical data that allow goals and objectives to be established for a comprehensive guidance program.

- A. Base assessments
- B. Needs assessment
- C. Informal assessments
- D. Portfolios

Answer:

QUESTION 93

A school counselor has been informed that there are approximately 150 students without lockers due to availability. The school counselor will need to make a decision as to what action to take. Which of the following data is less likely needed to make an informed decision?

- A. total number of lockers
- B. total number of students
- C. total number of broken lockers
- D. total number of occupied lockers

Answer:

Using the following data to answer the next two questions.

Elementary Education – Grade 6

Summary of Student Performance for Core Subject Areas

- Reading Scores:
    o 85% of the students are performing below average
    o 65% of the struggling students are English Language Learners
    o 5% of the students are performing above average
- Math Scores
    o 87% of the students are performing below average
    o 5% of the struggling students are English Language Learners
    o 7% of the students are performing above average
- Writing Scores
    o 90% of the students are performing below average
    o 75% of the struggling students are English Language Learners
    o 6% of the students are performing above average

QUESTION 94

Which of the following is NOT supported by the data?

A. English Language Learners are doing better in reading than writing.
B. English Language Learners need help in reading and writing.
C. Non-English Language Learners need help mostly in math.
D. All students need help in at least one subject area.

Answer:

QUESTION 95

I. discussing with teacher on better supporting several students
II. counseling in a small-group afterschool
III. helping students develop personal goals

Of the above, which of the following is/are direct student services that a school counselor can provide?

A. I only
B. I and II
C. II and III
D. I, II, and III

Answer:

QUESTION 96

Which of the following is the greatest need for improvement based on the data?

A. improvement in writing for nearly all students
B. improvement in reading for English Language Learners
C. improvement in grammar for nearly all students
D. improvement in math for non-English Language Learners

Answer:

QUESTION 97

Goal of Elementary Education:
Ensuring all students has equitable access to learning curriculum.

The school counselor is seeking to determine how well this goal is being achieved. Which of the following approaches would be the best to implement?

A. visiting classrooms while teachers are instructing
B. analyzing culture background of students who have improved
C. reviewing disaggregated results from several recent assessments
D. discussing with students about recent lessons instructed by the teacher

Answer:

QUESTION 98

The school counselor has noticed a school trend toward declining math scores on statewide assessments. The school counselor desires to plan professional development activities to address the problem. Which of the following is the best first action to take during the planning process?

A. interview teachers to see what methods are currently being used
B. organize a team of teachers to come up with professional development activities
C. analyze test results to understand specific math skills requiring improvement and subgroups of students requiring additional support
D. analyze test results of previous years with excellent performance on statewide assessments and understand the methods used during instruction at the time

Answer:

QUESTION 99

The Family Educational Rights and Privacy Act of 1974 give parents/guardians of a minor who is getting special needs services the right to

A. remove their child from standardize exams.
B. obtain educational records to share with non-school individuals.
C. select special education services.
D. opt out of IEP meetings.

Answer:

QUESTION 100

Which of the following is a type of test score that indicates a student's relative position among a group of students in the same grade who are tested at the same time?

A. raw score
B. average score
C. percentile rank
D. composite score

Answer:

QUESTION 101

A description of the student's current academic achievement level and functional performance is required by:

A. Daily Assessment Records
B. IEP
C. IFSP
D. 504 Plan

Answer:

QUESTION 102

A school counselor has notice that too many elementary education students at a K-6th grade-level school are bringing cell phones to school. Which of the following is the best and appropriate approach to resolve the problem?

A. have metal dictators daily when students enter the school
B. not to return confiscated cell phones back to students or parents
C. implement a harsher punishment for students who bring cell phones
D. send a letter to inform parents of cell phone policy and have parents sign the letter

Answer:

QUESTION 103

A school counselor has notice that certain eighth-grade students, such as ELLs and students with an economically disadvantaged classification, tend to perform much lower than their peers on assignments. Which of the following professional development activity is the best for the teachers to undertake to support struggling students?

- A. establishing assessments that are tailored to struggling students
- B. providing differentiated instruction that builds on students' strength
- C. reviewing instructional methods that have worked with some students
- D. understanding different ways of learning in different countries and cultures

Answer:

QUESTION 104

A school surveys students about their interests in subject areas; the students' responses matter because they are?

- A. relevant
- B. valid
- C. measurable
- D. consistent

Answer:

QUESTION 105

Strengthening instructional decision making is best done by which with of the following?

- A. having access to wide range data on students' assessment for different grade levels
- B. having understanding of students' background information
- C. having access to updated worksheets and lesson plans
- D. having understanding of current standards

Answer:

QUESTION 106

A school counselor, a principal, and grade level teachers are getting together to discuss math scores to improve scores for the following school year. What kind of meeting are they holding?

A. school improvement planning
B. grade level planning
C. teacher development planning
D. district improvement planning

Answer:

QUESTION 107

A school counselor is approached by a parent who is displeased about instruction relating to world religions that is included in history class. Which of the following described by the parent should be the most concerning to the school counselor?

A. questioning the existence of God
B. promoting one religion to be more worthy than another
C. having students to learn about practices of different religions
D. allowing students to share information about their own religion

Answer:

QUESTION 108

Which of the following is strictly considered morally unethical?

A. School counselor is taking money from the school operating budget to buy personal items.
B. School counselor using staff time to create worksheets to market online for personal gain.
C. School counselor refusing to provide information to parents regarding his child's grades.
D. School counselor seeking donations for school events from local businesses.

Answer:

QUESTION 109

At a high school, the graduation rate is very high, but the number of students applying to college is 50% of the graduating rate. Which of the following is the best way to increase college admission?

A. educate the students about opportunities associated with obtaining a college education
B. give students fee waivers, so they don't have to pay for college application fee
C. support students in preparation for SAT and ACT exams
D. provide students with support in applying for colleges

Answer:

QUESTION 110

Which of the following is the best type of assessment to provide useful feedback for professional development?

A. circular assessment
B. formative assessment
C. summative assessment
D. quantitative assessment

Answer:

QUESTION 111

I. evaluating data to make decision on achieving vision and goals
II. aligning all resources, including technology to achieve the vision
III. outlining criteria to show how instructional programs support the vision

Which of the following are needed to ensure continuous improvement toward the vision and goals of schools?

A. I and II
B. I and III
C. II and III
D. I, II, and III

Answer:

QUESTION 112

The Individuals with Disabilities Education Improvement Act (IDEA)

A. forces federal government to provide federal funding for early childhood programs.
B. requires states to create early intervention programs.
C. requires schools to have funding for improving technology for early childhood special education students.
D. requires states to provide data to the federal government on student progress in core academic areas.

Answer:

QUESTION 113

In decision making process concerning curriculum, the group that is not needed is _____.

A. curriculum experts
B. professional staff
C. school counselors
D. parents

Answer:

QUESTION 114

Which of the following is the primary purpose of scaffolding student learning?

A. ensure students' learning
B. assist students to become independent learners
C. encourage positive group engagement
D. assist students in independently completing assessment

Answer:

QUESTION 115

An open school event is being held at an elementary school. Which of the following is the most effective strategy for showing respect to and sensitivity to the cultural diversity among the families?

    A. have staff to translate for necessary families
    B. have written communication in multiple languages
    C. have staff to support students with disabilities
    D. have student-made posters of different cultures around the school

Answer:

QUESTION 116

Which of the following is the best way for a school counselor to reduce his or her workload?

    A. add more support staff
    B. delegate responsibilities
    C. work during lunch hour
    D. focus on major issues

Answer:

QUESTION 117

What is the maximum number of days a special education student can be suspended?

    A. 3 days
    B. 5 days
    C. 10 days
    D. 15 days

Answer:

QUESTION 118

Which of the following is needed to make an informed decision regarding school dilemmas?

A. data
B. support
C. options
D. alternatives

Answer:

QUESTION 119

A school counselor is very unhappy with a new district policy. The school counselor has expressed her concern to the district, but the district stands by the policy. The school counselor should

A. ignore the policy.
B. follow the policy.
C. get parents to express concern.
D. continue to contest the policy.

Answer:

QUESTION 120

The school counselor is reaching out to members of various demographic groups that make up the school community to support in playing an active role in the school. The school counselor's action best demonstrates

A. gaining support for success.
B. getting different ideas to ensure success.
C. supporting school success by valuing diversity.
D. ensuring that the community is involved in school decision making process.

Answer:

QUESTION 121

For the school year, the district has adopted new standards, and students are going to be tested on those standards for the upcoming statewide assessments. Towards the end of the school year, more and more parents are opting their child out of the assessment. In this situation, what is the most appropriate action for the school counselor to undertake?

- A. inform parents that students have been exposed to these standards for some time and the school has prepared the students
- B. inform parents that standards are going to be updated to meet the needs of the future
- C. deny the parents request to opt students out of the assessment
- D. convey the benefits of the assessments to the parents

Answer:

QUESTION 122

Which of the following is the most important question to answer when using community resources for school purposes?

- A. Are there enough resources to impact the entire school?
- B. Do the resources meet the needs of the school?
- C. Have these resources been used in the past?
- D. What are the limitations of the resources?

Answer:

QUESTION 123

The school counselor has notice that there are many English Language Learners (ELL) at the school. In reviewing the students' records, most of the students have been classified as ELL for over 5 years. Why is this concerning?

- A. The school does not have assessment tools to determine if ELL learners are ready to go into regular classrooms.
- B. There is nothing concerning about students being classified as ELL for over 5 years.
- C. The school will need more ELL teachers, which might be difficult to recruit.
- D. The students are not being taught effectively to come out of ELL classrooms.

Answer:

QUESTION 124

   I. Cognitive behavioral play therapy involves child in counseling play.
   II. Cognitive behavioral play therapy is open ended.
   III. Cognitive behavioral play therapy allows development of adaptive thoughts and behaviors.

Cognitive behavioral play therapy places a very strong emphasis on the student's involvement in the process of developing appropriate social skills. Of the above, which of the following are properties of cognitive behavioral play therapy?

   A. I and II
   B. I and III
   C. II and III
   D. I, II, and III

Answer:

QUESTION 125

To improve organization within the school system, the most important factor in sampling public opinion about education is:

   A. population size
   B. sample size
   C. random size
   D. representativeness of sample

Answer:

QUESTION 126

A middle school is seeking to start a program by getting talented, skilled community members to communicate the importance of learning or to speak at assemblies. To ensure the program is the best, which of the following factor should be given the highest priority?

    A. the number of years of experience the individuals have in their field of expertise
    B. the number of awards the individuals have in their field of expertise
    C. the relevance of the individuals' experience to the school curriculum
    D. the relevance of the individuals having a degree related to their job

Answer:

QUESTION 127

Which of the following is the most important issue to correct when it comes to the school safety and security?

    A. multiple entrances that are unmonitored
    B. metal detectors that were installed years ago
    C. emergency procedures reviewed over 5 years ago
    D. new teachers not trained for emergency response

Answer:

QUESTION 128

Which of the following will receive the greatest consideration in establishing comprehensive program for student activities in schools?

    A. needs of the facilities
    B. input from school staff
    C. the staffing requirements
    D. developmental needs of the students

Answer:

QUESTION 129

A school counselor will be engaging staff member to select activities for the upcoming school year for parents and students to participate. Which of the following is the most important question to consider to ensure effective decision making?

   A. Will the activities allow all the students and parents to participate?
   B. What resources will be required for the activities?
   C. Will the activities be within the defined budget?
   D. Will the activities reflect the school goals?

Answer:

QUESTION 130

One of the middle school students in Mr. Matt science class stated "Why can't I just pay you to give me good grades like Mr. Bark in math class?" The science teacher informs the school counselor of what was said by the student. Which of the following is the best action for the school counselor to take?

   A. tell the teacher to inform the principal
   B. talk to the student who made the statement
   C. review grades given by the math teacher to see irregularities
   D. nothing as this is just a student making a statement with no proof

Answer:

QUESTION 131

I. Access by minors to inappropriate matter on the Internet and World Wide Web
II. The safety and security of minors when using electronic mail, chat rooms, and other forms of direct electronic communications
III. Unauthorized access including "hacking" and other unlawful activities by minors online
IV. Unauthorized disclosure, use, and dissemination of personal information regarding minors

Of the above, which of the following are addressed by the Children's Internet Protection Act (CIPA)?

A. I only
B. I and II
C. II, and III
D. I, II, III, and IV

Answer:

QUESTION 132

I. suspend the boy for five days
II. conduct a meeting with the boy's parents
III. have the boy complete bullying prevention training with the school counselor

A seventh girl has informed the school counselor that a boy in her class has been verbally bullying her for the past month. The boy has said that the girl is fat, smelly, and ugly. The boy has confessed to this. Which of the following is/are the action(s) to take?

A. I only
B. I and II
C. I and III
D. II and III

Answer:

QUESTION 133

Having a strong school organization requires a good decision-making process. For school counselors the decision making process involves all the following except?

A. understanding the problem
B. considering views of opposing staff
C. remaining firm with decisions
D. having a unbiased mindset

Answer:

QUESTION 134

The goal of a group is to improve parents' involvement in students' learning and performance. The group has developed the plan and is in the process of implementing the plan to involve parents. Which of the following needs to be undertaken to ensure that the plan is effective?

A. have parents complete a survey on the plan
B. track the number of parents involved
C. track students' performance
D. ensure the objective of the plan is communicated

Answer:

QUESTION 135

Jenny is a school counselor at a local elementary school. One of her goals for the new school year is to ensure all individuals have an environment that shows commitment to the belief that all individuals can learn and succeed. Jenny can best support this vision across the school, by having teachers value which classroom practice?

A. use various instructional method to support all students in classroom throughout the year
B. provide monthly engagement to obtain input from students and teachers on what works and what does not work
C. ensure that state standards are being following to ensure excellence in performance base testing
D. having more interactive and fun educational activities and field trips

Answer:

QUESTION 136

Communication is vital part in ensuring robust school organization. Communication among group members is connected to which of the following?

- A. relationship
- B. trust
- C. organization
- D. conformity

Answer:

QUESTION 137

To ensure mission of school organization expectations are consistent, goals need to be all the following except:

- A. clear
- B. accepted
- C. attainable
- D. measurable

Answer:

QUESTION 138

Which of the following types of behavior best shows a school counselor's sensitivity to the needs of an organization?

- A. opening an anonymous survey for teacher
- B. conducting engagement sessions with school staff
- C. ensuring multiple family engagement with parents and staff
- D. establishing two way communication with responding to needs

Answer:

QUESTION 139

Which of the following is the main purpose of involving students, parents, and teachers in the education decision-making process in schools?

A. obtain various inputs from different groups
B. prevent groups from dominating decisions
C. ensure proper representation of individuals
D. ensure involvement of all stakeholders

Answer:

QUESTION 140

Special education programs are populated with students from particular cultural background and language background. School counselors need to take which of the following approach to ensure proper identification of individuals entering the special education program?

A. conduct interviews to confirm students need to be in the special education program
B. have assessment tools that take into consideration that students are from different backgrounds from language and culture standpoint.
C. use proper assessment processes with students prior to being identified as special education student
D. review the placement procedures currently used to determine if the student grade level is correct

Answer:

QUESTION 141

The school counselor has abruptly decided to resign. The position is vacant and will take several weeks or perhaps a month to fill. What is the best action for the school to take?

A. ask the state to send a temporary school counselor
B. hold off on discussing students' issues until a replacement is found
C. review current staff to see who has the best qualification to temporary provide school counselor support
D. have the school physiologist fill the position of the school counselor

Answer:

QUESTION 142

Which of the following is the least effective way for elementary students to learn content?

- A. lecture
- B. cooperative learning
- C. direct instruction
- D. modeling

Answer:

QUESTION 143

  I. coming to school very irritable
  II. being hyperactive most of the day
  III. fighting with other children

The first step the school counselor needs to take in this situation is to:

- A. refer the student to the school nurse for deficit/hyperactivity disorder symptoms
- B. monitor the behavior for few months to discuss with the principal
- C. discuss with parents on home behavior
- D. develop an intervention plan to support the student

Answer:

QUESTION 144

Blake is a new student from another state, and he has separation anxiety. At the beginning of class during circle time, he does not want to let his father go. The best action for the teacher is to:

- A. have the father come visit Blake a couple of times per day
- B. have the father remain with Blake for 15 minutes and, then, ask him to leave
- C. have the father participate in circle time, and when Blake is involved, have the parent sneak out of the room
- D. introduce Blake to two friends and ask him to sit between them and engage in a discussion

Answer:

QUESTION 145

Which statement would be classified as a long term goal rather than a course or lesson objective?

A. The student will analyze independently informational text.
B. The student will be able to identify the verbs in a paragraph.
C. The student will be able to develop a well organized presentation.
D. The student will be able to identify main ideas.

Answer:

QUESTION 146

A school counselor has been working at a school for three months. After evaluating the needs of the district, the school counselor has been informed that she will have to go to another school. The school counselor refuses this move, and she takes action to abandon the position without in advance notification. The school counselor has:

A. inappropriately abandon the position
B. the right to abandon the position
C. taken appropriate action
D. breached the contract

Answer:

QUESTION 147

IDEA covers which of the following disabilities from birth:

I. cerebral palsy
II. visual impairment
III. Down syndrome
IV. hearing impairment

A. I and III
B. II and IV
C. I and II
D. III and IV

Answer:

QUESTION 148

A school counselor overhears a student picking on another student. The student says "you look very ugly with glasses." What is the best phrase for the school counselor to say to the student doing the picking?

   A. we treat all of our classmates with respect
   B. we all look different, it's no need to point it out
   C. we do not want to be mean to others
   D. glasses are to help people see better

Answer:

QUESTION 149

   I.   parents
   II. regular education teacher(s)
   III. special education teacher(s)

According to IDEA 2004, an IEP team meeting consists of which of the following from above?

   A. I and II
   B. I and III
   C. II and III
   D. I, II, and III

Answer:

QUESTION 150

A four-year-old uses both English and Spanish languages at home. Discussing with the school counselor, the grandfather expressed concerns that his child sometimes mixes up words between the two languages. Which of the following would be the best response for the school counselor to provide the grandfather?

   A. document instances of the child mixing words to see if patterns exist
   B. inform the grandfather that this will continue for many years to come
   C. inform grandfather that this is common for the child's age
   D. conduct a formal assessment for placement of special education services

Answer:

School Counselor Exam - Correct Answer Sheet

Below is an optional answer sheet to use to document answers.

Question Number	Right Answer	Question Number	Right Answer	Question Number	Right Answer	Question Number	Right Answer	Question Number	Right Answer
1	C	31	A	61	C	91	B	121	A
2	C	32	D	62	B	92	B	122	B
3	C	33	A	63	B	93	D	123	D
4	A	34	C	64	B	94	D	124	B
5	C	35	C	65	D	95	C	125	D
6	C	36	B	66	D	96	A	126	C
7	A	37	C	67	A	97	C	127	A
8	C	38	C	68	C	98	C	128	C
9	A	39	A	69	C	99	B	129	D
10	A	40	C	70	B	100	C	130	A
11	A	41	A	71	A	101	B	131	D
12	C	42	B	72	C	102	D	132	D
13	B	43	C	73	C	103	B	133	C
14	B	44	D	74	B	104	A	134	B
15	D	45	A	75	C	105	A	135	A
16	D	46	D	76	C	106	A	136	B
17	A	47	A	77	B	107	B	137	B
18	B	48	C	78	B	108	B	138	D
19	C	49	C	79	D	109	D	139	A
20	B	50	A	80	C	110	B	140	C
21	D	51	D	81	B	111	D	141	C
22	A	52	A	82	C	112	B	142	A
23	D	53	B	83	C	113	D	143	D
24	B	54	B	84	B	114	B	144	D
25	B	55	C	85	C	115	A	145	A
26	B	56	B	86	C	116	B	146	D
27	D	57	D	87	D	117	C	147	A
28	D	58	B	88	C	118	A	148	A
29	C	59	C	89	D	119	B	149	D
30	B	60	D	90	C	120	C	150	C

NOTE: Getting approximately 80% of the questions correct increases chances of obtaining passing score on the real exam. This varies from different states and university programs.

This page is intentionally left blank.

Practice Exam Questions and Explanation – School Counselor

QUESTION 1

A student's father called the school counselor and told the counselor that his son had shared with him that one of his friends was being physically abused. The school counselor met with the boy in question; however, he denied being abused. As a school counselor, which of the following is the best action to pursue further?

- A. do nothing as the boy denied the physical abuse
- B. continue to investigate to confirm if abuse occurred
- C. report the suspected child abuse per state law
- D. involve the school principal to discuss with the boy

Answer: C

Explanation: State laws require the school counselor to report the suspicion of child abuse. Being aware of potential child abuse and not reporting the abuse, the counselor can be fine or even sent to jail in some states. The safest and best action is to report the information to the appropriate agency per state law.

QUESTION 2

A student has informed the school counselor that she thinks she is pregnant and plans to get an abortion without telling her parents. Which of the following is the first question that the school counselor should inquire?

- A. Was the sex consensual?
- B. How old is the father of the baby?
- C. Did you confirm that you are pregnant?
- D. How is your relationship with your parent?

Answer: C

Explanation: In the question, it states that the student "thinks" she is pregnant. The first step is to know for sure if the student is pregnant. The counselor needs to ask if the student has confirmed the pregnancy. Other questions are relevant, but the first question to ask is Option C.

QUESTION 3

A student has recently told the school counselor that she cuts herself. The cuts shown do not indicate that the student is suicidal. Which of the following is the best first action to take in this situation?

- A. contact child protective services
- B. contact the parents to help solve the problem
- C. understand the reasoning for the cutting behavior
- D. enroll the student in therapy sessions with the school psychologist

Answer: C

Explanation: As indicated in the question, the cuts are not suicidal, so contacting the parents is not the best first action. Option A and C are unnecessary if the cuts are non-suicidal. The counselor needs to understand the reasoning for the cutting behavior and to put a plan to get the student support.

QUESTION 4

Which of the following court cases consistently found that school counselors did not "owe a legal duty" to prevent a student's suicide?

- A. Eisel vs. Montgomery County Board of Education of 1991
- B. James vs. American School Counselor Association of 2001
- C. Eisel vs. American School Counselor Association of 2001
- D. James vs. Montgomery County Board of Education of 1991

Answer: A

Explanation: Eisel vs. Montgomery County Board of Education of 1991 consistently found that school counselors did not "owe a legal duty" to prevent a student's suicide.

QUESTION 5

A student has threatened suicide and likely going to commit suicide. The school counselors' legal liability ends when

- A. the student gets help.
- B. the counselor recommends appropriate action to teachers.
- C. the counselor recommends appropriate action to school officials.
- D. the student is put on suicide watch.

Answer: C

Explanation: A school counselors' legal liability concludes when school officials or parents have been informed that a student is at risk and appropriate action has been recommended.

QUESTION 6

Jenny is the school counselor at a small high school. Her daughter is planning to attend the same school next year. If the daughter has personal issues to discuss, as the school counselor, Jenny's best action is to:

- A. provide school counseling services to her daughter
- B. provide parenting advice to her daughter
- C. seek outside consultation for her daughter
- D. request principal to support her daughter

Answer: C

Explanation: Since the daughter is needing counseling related to a personal matter, the best approach for Jenny is to seek outside school consultation for her daughter. This will avoid any unethical dual relationship.

QUESTION 7

Which of the following best describes appropriate note taking for school counselors?

- A. minimal notes, containing student name, time and a few details as a memory aid
- B. minimal notes, containing student name, time and a many details
- C. notes containing student name, problem, and treatment plan
- D. minimal notes, containing student name, time and a treatment plan

Answer: A

Explanation: Treatment plans do not need to be included in notes for school counselors, so options C and D are eliminated. Having many details is not recommended for notes, so option B is eliminated. Option A best describes appropriate note taking for school counselors.

QUESTION 8

Family Education Rights and Privacy Act (FERPA) gives parents the right to see all of the following except

- A. standardize test scores.
- B. report card grades.
- C. notes taken by school counselors.
- D. all of the above.

Answer: C

Explanation: Family Education Rights and Privacy Act does not give parents the right to see notes taken by school counselors.

QUESTION 9

A school is planning to have a group of students complete multiple assessments to determine if they are classified as gifted and talented. In respect to the data obtained from the assessment, the school counselor's role is to

   A. analyze data.
   B. administer test.
   C. collect data.
   D. coordinate test.

Answer: A

Explanation: School counselors are involved in the analysis of data obtained from different assessments. They are not responsible for the coordination, collection and/or administration of the any assessment used in the selection process.

QUESTION 10

A school counselor is helping all students by getting them to:

- develop a portfolio to show strengths and interests
- apply strategies to accomplish future academic and career success
- show the connection between coursework and life experiences

These actions best describe the school counselor helping students

   A. get ready for college.
   B. get ready to go to high school.
   C. get ready to help student decide on a career.
   D. get ready for senior year of high school education.

Answer: A

Explanation: The school counselor is getting the students ready for college. Showing strengths and interests are related to getting into college. Applying strategies for future academics along with showing the connection between coursework and life experiences relate to getting ready for college.

QUESTION 11

Which of the following is critical to ensure a positive effect the school counselor and the school counseling program have on students and school stakeholders?

- A. school counselor performance evaluation
- B. confidentiality
- C. annual school goals
- D. high scores on standardize tests

Answer: A

Explanation: Having a school counselor performance evaluation will allow the determination of how effective the program is to the students and staff.

QUESTION 12

In regards to bullying, the school counselor's role include all the following except?

- A. collaborating with others to promote safe schools and confront issues
- B. encourage the development of policies supporting a safe school environment
- C. punish students who are engaging in bullying acts
- D. provide leadership in implementing school-wide prevention programs

Answer: C

Explanation: The school counselor's responsibility is not to punish students who are engaging in bullying acts; punishing is for the principal or the assistant principal to undertake.

QUESTION 13

_____ is when schools along with social institutions and parents support the positive character development of children and adults.

- A. Development
- B. Character education
- C. School counseling program
- D. Positive relationship

Answer: B

Explanation: Character education is when schools along with social institutions and parents support the positive character development of children and adults.

QUESTION 14

- I. increased risk of child abuse
- II. erosion of trust between an adult and child
- III. adverse effects on cognitive development

All of the above best describe negative effects of which of the following?

- A. Family problems
- B. Corporal punishment
- C. Drinking
- D. Neglect

Answer: B

Explanation: Corporal punishment can result in increased risk of child abuse, increased antisocial behavior, erosion of trust between an adult and child, increased likelihood of depression, and adverse effects on cognitive development.

QUESTION 15

Using behavioral contracts, setting realistic expectations, enforcing rules consistently, and emphasizing positive behaviors of students are alternatives to which of the following?

A. suspending
B. retaining
C. expelling
D. whipping

Answer: D

Explanation: Using behavioral contracts, setting realistic expectations, enforcing rules consistently, and emphasizing positive behaviors of students are best alternatives to whipping (corporal punishment).

QUESTION 16

Which of the following is a way for a school counselor to foster increased awareness, understanding and appreciation of cultural diversity in the school?

A. teach tolerance
B. address issues of nonviolence
C. discuss social justice
D. all of the above

Answer: D

Explanation: All of the choices can be related to fostering increase awareness, understanding and appreciation of cultural diversity in the school.

QUESTION 17

Disruptive student behavior is one of the most significant, ongoing problems confronting schools. To establish and maintain safe and respectful learning environments, school counselors must ensure

- A. effective discipline programs.
- B. rules are being clearly communicated.
- C. constructed feedback to students
- D. teachers are trained to handle disruptive behavior

Answer: A

Explanation: Having effective discipline programs that maintain nonthreatening relationships with students and allows appropriate punishment for disruptive behavior is critical to establish and maintain safe and respectful learning environments.

QUESTION 18

A school counselor must recognize that _____ have encountered barriers to participating in a rigorous curriculum and higher level classes.

- A. African Americans
- B. underrepresented populations
- C. young children
- D. special education students with severe disability

Answer: B

Explanation: The best answer that fills the blank is underrepresented populations. Special education students with severe disability will likely not be exposed to rigorous curriculum.

QUESTION 19

Which of the following is not within the scope of a school counselor's responsibility?

- A. individual counseling
- B. group counseling
- C. therapy addressing psychological disorders
- D. respond to student mental health crises

Answer: C

Explanation: A school counselor is not responsible for providing therapy or long-term counseling in schools to address psychological disorders.

QUESTION 20

Which of the following is not appropriate for a school counselor to undertake when working with a LGBTQ (lesbian, gay, bisexual, transgender and questioning) student?

- A. promote academic achievement
- B. encourage the student to select a certain identity
- C. counsel students with feelings about their sexual orientation
- D. encourage the student not to be violent when confronted with bullying

Answer: B

Explanation: The question ask for an action that is not appropriate by the school counselor. The school counselor should not encourage the student to select a certain identify. This should be done independently by the student at the appropriate time.

QUESTION 21

I. parents
II. teachers
III. students

School counselors are skilled in both educating and counseling, allowing them to function as a facilitator among which of the following from above?

A. I and II
B. I and III
C. II and III
D. I, II, and III

Answer: D

Explanation: School counselors are trained in both educating and counseling, allowing them to function as a facilitator between parents, teachers and students in matters concerning the students' learning, abilities and any areas requiring improvement.

QUESTION 22

Which of the following best completes the statement below?

School counselors provide services to _____.

A. all students
B. students in need
C. all school members
D. students and family members

Answer: A

Explanation: School counselors provide services to students in needs, but they also provide services to those not in need. The best answer is option A.

QUESTION 23

All of the following are types of behavior therapy interventions except:

- A. systematic desensitization
- B. flooding
- C. aversion conditioning
- D. therapeutic transference

Answer: D

Explanation: Therapeutic transference is a psychodynamic intervention, whereas the others are behavioral.

QUESTION 24

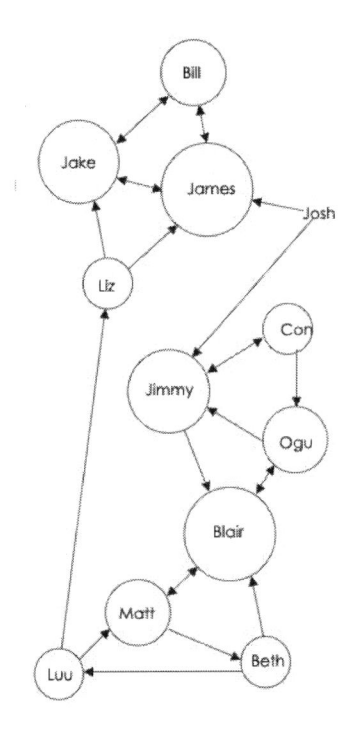

A school counselor could best use the sociogram shown above to assess which of the following elements of sixth-grade students' social development?

- A. popularity
- B. peer acceptance
- C. development
- D. communication skills

Answer: B

Explanation: Sociograms illustrate interactions and relationship preferences within a group of people. A school counselor could best use the sociogram shown above to assess peer acceptance.

QUESTION 25

Matt is a 10-year-old Caucasian male. He was referred to the school counselor, Ms. Blake, by Ms. James, his 4th-grade teacher, who has noticed ongoing behavioral problems in class. Matt is unable to focus, does not listen, and has difficulty communicating with classmates. Ms. Blake has observed the student on the playground having difficulty interacting with his peers. As the school counselor, Ms. Blake next best option is which of the following?

  A. recommend to visit a doctor to see if he has Attention Deficit Hyperactivity Disorder
  B. contact the parent to understand the behavior displayed outside of school
  C. have the student participate in weekly discussion with the school counselor
  D. recommend the student be placed in special education classes

Answer: B

Explanation: The school counselor should contact the parent(s) to discuss the behavior and gain understanding on how the student is behaving at home. This will allow the school counselor to understand the extent of the behavioral issues.

QUESTION 26

A school counselor has observed a student constantly describing objects such as buses and chairs as having feelings and other lifelike properties. Which of the following of Jean Piaget's concepts is best shown by this behavior?

  A. artificialism
  B. animism
  C. conservation
  D. equilibrium

Answer: B

Explanation: When a child assigns lifelike properties to inanimate objects, the child is showing Jean Piaget's concept of animism.

QUESTION 27

During a classroom guidance lesson, an elementary school counselor assists a student by focusing on tasks that a child can perform with the help and guidance of others but cannot yet perform independently. Providing such assistance is best related to which of Lev Vygotsky's concept?

A. scaffolding
B. differentiation
C. intersubjectivity
D. zone of proximal development

Answer: D

Explanation: The zone of proximal development (ZPD) is an critical principle of Lev Vygotsky's theory. ZPD is the range of tasks that a child can perform with the assistance of others but cannot yet perform independently.

QUESTION 28

Which of the following is considered an external referral in regards to school counseling services?

A. teachers
B. nurses
C. peers
D. parents

Answer: D

Explanation: Parents are not directly included in the school system, so any referral by parents is considered external.

QUESTION 29

Several first grade teachers approached the school counselor with concerns that their students are having behavior issues. Issues include refusing to share, pushing each other, and calling each other names. To support the teachers, the school counselor plans to implement classroom guidance lessons focused on teaching social skills to all first grade students. Of the following, which is the best way for the teacher to develop appropriate curriculum for the first grade students?

- A. Search the Internet for lesson plans developed by other counselors.
- B. Ask teachers to develop the lesson plan and make necessary changes.
- C. Review professional materials and ASCA website.
- D. Use previous year lessons related to anger management.

Answer: C

Explanation: Professional material and ASCA website will provide the most reliable information to develop appropriate curriculum for the first grade students.

QUESTION 30

Several first grade teachers approached the school counselor with concerns that their students are having behavior issues. Issues include refusing to share, pushing each other, and calling each other names. To support the teachers, the school counselor plans to implement classroom guidance lessons focused on teaching social skills to all first grade students. After delivering the lesson to the first grade students, which of the following is the best secondary intervention approach?

- A. individual coaching
- B. small-group counseling
- C. student-parent counseling
- D. psychoeducational group counseling

Answer: B

Explanation: Once the counselor has given the lesson to the students, the best approach is to do small-group counseling. Option A will be time consuming for the counselor. Option C and D do not make sense in this situation.

QUESTION 31

A student has approached the school counselor for a letter of recommendation for a college application. The counselor has agreed to provide a letter of recommendation, in which the counselor writes about the student's good academic standing, honest behavior, and commitment to succeed. Several weeks later, the counselor finds out that the student has fabricated some parts of the personal essay for the college application. The school counselor is obligated to

- A. do nothing in this situation.
- B. retract the letter of recommendation.
- C. require the student to re-submit the personal essay.
- D. inform the college of the fabricated parts of the personal essay.

Answer: A

Explanation: The school counselor is obligated to do nothing in this situation. Sometimes students do fabricated some parts of the personal essay for college applications; it is not good practice. However, the counselor is not obligated to take any action.

QUESTION 32

John, a ninth-grade student, has committed suicide on school property. As the school counselor, which of the following is not an action to take during the first few days of this tragic event?

- A. provide moral support to the students
- B. engage with parents on supporting students
- C. conduct group counseling with students close to John
- D. investigate the reasons for the student committing suicide

Answer: D

Explanation: The school counselor's responsibility is to support the student population to deal with this tragic event. Option A, B, and C relate to the school counselor appropriately supporting the students. Option D is not an action the school counselor should undertake.

QUESTION 33

    I.   strong reading skills and large vocabulary

    II.   strong motivation to be focused in particular area

    III.   strong communication skills with peers

Of the above, which of the following are clear indication(s) of a gifted child?

    A. I only
    B. I and II
    C. I and III
    D. I, II, and III

Answer: A

Explanation: The keyword in the question is "clear." Strong reading skills and large vocabulary is a clear indication of a gifted child. Strong communication skills and strong motivation can be displayed by individuals who are not gifted.

QUESTION 34

_____ is an effective and efficient way to deliver direct services to students in which a counselor works with multiple students simultaneously to address common concerns or problem behavior.

    A. School counseling curriculum
    B. Therapy counseling
    C. Group counseling
    D. Pair counseling

Answer: C

Explanation: Group counseling is an effective and efficient way to deliver direct services to students in which a counselor works with multiple students simultaneously to address common concerns or problem behavior.

QUESTION 35

A school counselor has been working with a student for several months regarding communication and behavioral issues. The counselor has not seen any progress since she started working with the student. Which of the following is the best approach to take next?

- A. send the student to the school psychologist
- B. have the student work with external counselor
- C. have the student work with another internal counselor
- D. have the student work with the special education department

Answer: C

Explanation: The school counselor has seen no progress since working with the student. The next best approach to take is have another school counselor support the student to see if progress can be achieved.

QUESTION 36

Which of the following is not a post-action after a serious crisis has occurred on school property?

- A. Reassure individuals that the world is a good place, however that there are people who do bad things.
- B. Keep all information from the kids to prevent them from becoming scared.
- C. Ensure attachments and relationships.
- D. Listen to individuals' fears and concerns.

Answer: B

Explanation: The best approach is to be honest with individuals and share with them as much information as they are developmentally able to handle.

QUESTION 37

Which of the following is not an external consultee?

- A. tutors
- B. parents
- C. school nurse
- D. agency personal

Answer: C

Explanation: School nurse is considered an internal consultee.

QUESTION 38

The ASCA National Model: A Framework for School Counseling Programs addresses which of the three domains?

- A. individual, small-group, and large-group classroom guidance
- B. communication, communities, and collaboration
- C. career, academic, and personal-social development
- D. foundations, accountability, and management

Answer: C

Explanation: The ASCA National Model: A Framework for School Counseling Programs career, academic, and personal-social development.

QUESTION 39

A ninth-grade student is going through a period of mild to moderate depression, in which the student is having negative views of self, the world in general, and the future. Which of the following is the best first approach for the school counselor to take?

- A. cognitive therapeutic approach
- B. refer to medical professional
- C. open-ended communication approach
- D. provide anxiety medication

Answer: A

Explanation: The keywords in the question are "mild to moderate" and "first approach." Since the depression is not severe, referring to medical professional is unnecessary. Option D is not something the school counselor can undertake. Option C makes no sense in this situation. Option A is the best approach as it is commonly used for depression as it is focused on identifying specific distortions in thinking and providing guidance on how to change this thinking.

QUESTION 40

Which of the following is NOT one of the major components of the ASCA National Model?

- A. foundation
- B. management
- C. performance
- D. accountability

Answer: C

Explanation: The ASCA National Model has four major components which include foundation, management, delivery, and accountability.

QUESTION 41

A middle school class is going on a field trip to the history museum. Information has surfaced that the bus has been in an accident in which three students are injured. As a member of the school's emergency response team, which of the following steps should the school counselor take first?

    A. confirm that the information surfacing is accurate
    B. ensure that the police and ambulances are on the location of the accident
    C. call the parents of all students to provide update on condition
    D. provide support to the students and teachers impacted by the accident

Answer: A

Explanation: Before any action is taken, all members of the emergency response team need to ensure the information provided is accurate. This will prevent confusion and chaos.

QUESTION 42

    I.   keeping clerical records
    II.   interpreting student records
    III.   computing grade-point averages

Of the above, which of the following is/are inappropriate for school counselors to undertake?

    A. I only
    B. I and II
    C. I and III
    D. I, II, and III

Answer: B

Explanation: According to the American School Counselor Association, keeping clerical records and interpreting records are inappropriate behavior of school counselors.

QUESTION 43

Which of the following is the first stage in Erik Erikson's theory of personality development?

A. autonomy vs. shame
B. intimacy vs. inferiority
C. trust vs. mistrust
D. ego integrity vs. despair

Answer: C

Explanation: The following are the stages in Erik Erikson's theory of personality development:

- trust vs. mistrust
- autonomy vs. shame
- initiative vs. guilt
- ego identity vs. role confusion
- intimacy vs. isolation
- generativity vs. stagnation
- ego integrity vs. despair

QUESTION 44

I. providing planning career advice
II. supporting poor performing students
III. giving substance abuse education

The above best describes a school counselor providing support to which of the following group of students?

A. early childhood
B. middle school
C. elementary
D. high school

Answer: D

Explanation: The key was "planning career advice," which is likely given more to high school students as they embark on their journey to college.

QUESTION 45

A high school counselor is seeking to implement technology in helping place students in their desired elective classes. Which of the following types of software would be the best to use?

- A. database
- B. word processing
- C. excel document
- D. adobe editor

Answer: A

Explanation: The school counselor is looking for a software that will help students in their desired elective classes. Of the courses, the database will support the school counselor in the best way.

QUESTION 46

A school counselor takes notes of discussion with students on a notepad. Ethical standards require that the counselor

- A. transfer the notes to a computer.
- B. memorize the notes and destroy the notes immediately.
- C. make a back up copy of the notes in case there are lost.
- D. establish a time limit for properly purging students' files.

Answer: D

Explanation: The school counselor's discussion with students might be sensitive, so having a time limit for properly purging students' files is the ethical action to take. This will protect the students information in the long term. Option B is not the answer as memorizing the notes is not practical with many students getting support.

QUESTION 47

Which of the following situations will require the school counselor to provide the longest duration support?

A. a fifth-grader who lost her father in a car accident
B. a teacher who lost her husband in a car accident
C. writing a student a letter of recommendation for a scholarship program
D. a student transitioning from special education class to general education class

Answer: A

Explanation: The question is asking about the longest duration of support the school counselor will need provided. When a child encounters a death of a parent, the process to grieve is lengthy. Of the choices, option A is the best option.

QUESTION 48

Which of the following provides protection to school counselors in case of any malpractice situations?

A. lobbying efforts
B. counselor union
C. liability insurance
D. professional development

Answer: C

Explanation: Liability insurance gives protection to school counselors in case of any malpractice situations. Not all activities are covered under liability insurance, but liability insurance is the only choice that provides protection to school counselors.

QUESTION 49

A student has come to the school counselor to talk about issues she is having since her father moved to another city and left her mother. It would likely be most critical to the student for the school counselor to

- A. keep conversation confidential.
- B. provide positive feedback.
- C. show respect for the family structure.
- D. provide hope for her father to return.

Answer: C

Explanation: Option A is something the school counselor will have to do as it is required by best practices and state laws. In addition, nothing in the question suggest the student will communicate something that will require disclosing the conversation. Also, option B is likely not possible as the situation is not positive. The counselor should not provide any hope for the father to return as the school counselor does not know. The family structure is different, so the school counselor should show respect for the family structure.

QUESTION 50

A school counselor is assisting a second grader deal with the death of her mother. As a school counselor, it is extremely critical to

- A. give the student the vocabulary to express her feelings
- B. provide the student with personal time during school time
- C. give examples of how the student should feel
- D. ensure the student this feeling is temporary

Answer: A

Explanation: The student is a second grader, who might have difficulty expressing herself. Early childhood students may not be able to recognize or label the appropriate emotions in certain situations. The school counselor can give the student vocabulary words to express her feelings.

QUESTION 51

I. increase job satisfaction
II. better manage time
III. increase productivity

Of the above, which of the following is/are reason for ensuring organization in school counseling programs?

A. I only
B. I and II
C. II and III
D. I, II, and III

Answer: D

Explanation: Organization of information and processes are critical for school counseling programs in reducing stress, helping better manage time, increasing productivity, promoting better quality of work, and increasing job satisfaction.

QUESTION 52

  I. analyzing disaggregated data
  II. assisting with duties in the principal's office
  III. coordinating achievement testing programs

Of the above, which of the following is/are appropriate behavior(s) for school counselors?

- A. I only
- B. I and II
- C. I and III
- D. I, II, and III

Answer: A

Explanation: According to the American School Counselor Association, school counselors can analyze disaggregated data. Assisting with duties in the principal's office and coordinating achievement testing programs are not within the scope of school counselors' job.

QUESTION 53

A school counselor is analyzing participation rates in Gifted and Talented courses by gender and determines that males are heavily represented in Math and Science courses but poorly represented in English. Which of the following is the most appropriate action for the counselor to undertake?

- A. balance the enrollment of males and females in Gifted and Talented courses
- B. review the procedures related to referring students to Gifted and Talented courses
- C. seek students who are interested in Gifted and Talented courses to balance the enrollment data
- D. share concerns with the principal to formally open an inquiry into Gifted and Talented enrollment process

Answer: B

Explanation: The issue presented in the data is related to enrollment in Gifted and Talented courses, so the best action for the counselor to take is to review the procedures related to referring students to Gifted and Talented courses.

QUESTION 54

A new school counselor has been hired at the local middle school. The school counselor comes from a wealthy family and previously worked in a private school. The middle school is located in a poor area, where annual income per family is less than $30,000. The crime rate in the location is higher than other surrounding areas. Which of the following is the best for the school counselor to undertake to better understand the environment the students are coming from?

- A. do online research on the community
- B. talk to students about life outside of school
- C. tour the streets and community
- D. attend open house at the school

Answer: B

Explanation: Option D is related to an open house, which is tailored to students' learning and progress; the focus is not learning about communities. Option C is not a good option as the crime rate is high; school counselors should not take this approach to learn more about communities. Talking to students about life outside of school will provide insight to the living environment and community. Option A is a good approach, but not the best approach.

QUESTION 55

Teachers are allowed to have emergency license to continue teaching temporary if they do not have all their certification exam passed; this is not the case for school counselors. Which of the following best explain the reason for this difference in expectations for teachers and school counselors when it comes to certification exams?

- A. there are few school counselors than teachers
- B. there is a higher demand for teachers
- C. school counselors deal with more sensitive matters
- D. school counselors exams are a lot easier than teachers exams

Answer: C

Explanation: School counselors deal with academic issues along with personal issues. In addition, school counselors might be involved in issues that are happening in students' homes. The skills require full certification to ensure the individual is fully ready and competent to handle the tasks associated with school counseling.

QUESTION 56

Which of the following is the best way for a school counselor to promote holistic student development?

- A. require teachers to have lessons geared toward holistic student development
- B. apply current research regarding nutrition and family systems
- C. have students fill survey on questions related to their home development
- D. give students the opportunity to express themselves

Answer: B

Explanation: Holistic education is the idea based on the premise that each person finds identity, meaning, and purpose in life through connections to the community or the natural world. The best for a school counselor to support students is applying current research regarding nutrition and family systems.

QUESTION 57

Which of the following is the best way for a school counselor to distribute information on scholarships and colleges for all students?

- A. email the information to all students
- B. place the information on bulletin near the cafeteria
- C. send the information to English teachers to distribute to students
- D. have a webpage on the school website related to college readiness

Answer: D

Explanation: The question asks how to distribute information on scholarships and colleges for all students. The keyword is "all." The best way to do that is Option D. Option A is not best practice as school officials should not be emailing students. Option C might not reach all students. Option B is not an effective way to put this information as it might be a lot of information.

QUESTION 58

Which of the following is likely the best topic that a school counselor can teach in a regular elementary school classroom setting?

- A. sex education
- B. anger management skills
- C. scientific inquiry process
- D. abortion

Answer: B

Explanation: The keywords in the question are "likely," "best," and "elementary." Option A and D are not grade appropriate. Neither is option C, but also Option C is not something a school counselor is going to teach. Option B is the best for the school counselor to teach in a regular elementary school classroom setting.

QUESTION 59

- I. addresses the immediate concerns of all students
- II. prevention and intervention
- III. school counselor role includes consulting and referring

The above describes which of the following Components of a Comprehensive School Counseling Program?

- A. Guidance Curriculum
- B. Individual Planning
- C. Responsive Services
- D. Monitoring Progress

Answer: C

Explanation: Responsive Services includes addressing immediate concerns. The purpose is to prevent and intervene on issues such as academic concerns, relationship concerns, abuse issues, family issues, etc.

QUESTION 60

A middle school counselor receives a call from the father of a student the counselor is supporting. The student has been unwilling in participating in school activities. The student has been talking to the counselor about his shyness, anxiety around peers, and negative self-concept. The father is aware of his son seeking support from the school counselor, and the father thanks the counselor for talking to his son. In addition, the father asks what his son has been talking about in the counseling sessions, and asks as to whether there is any way in which he can be supportive. Which of the following is the best action to take for the school counselor?

A. inform the father of the sessions and provide suggestion to what to do at home
B. inform in general terms what parents can do to be supportive without communicating details of the student's conversation
C. inform the father that he is not allowed to ask for information about what his son informed the school counselor
D. inform the father on the confidential nature of the counseling relationship between the counselor and student

Answer: D

Explanation: School counselors must keep confidentiality of conversation unless disclosure is required to prevent clear and imminent danger to the student or others. In this case, the best approach is to inform the father on the confidential nature of the counseling relationship between the counselor and student. Option C is a rude approach to communicate information to the father.

QUESTION 61

A first year reading teacher comes to the school counselor in misery because of the behavior of an extremely hyperactive student in her classroom. She has tried multiple strategies to get the student to behave appropriately, but she is not at her whit's end. She has not contacted the parents yet and the student has now been tested for ADHD. As a school counselor, which of the following is NOT the action to take in this situation?

- A. suggest the teacher provide more attention to the student during instruction
- B. integrate technology to calm the student down
- C. suggest that he be tested for ADHD
- D. suggest to provide incentives (ex. extra breaks) when working through lengthy tasks or activities

Answer: C

Explanation: As a school counselor, the action that is not appropriate is suggesting that the child be tested for ADHD as the school could be sued and have to pay for the testing/treatment. The special education department needs to be involved when discussing possible testing for ADHD.

QUESTION 62

There are three school counselors at a high school that supports nearly 500 students. One of the school counselors has decided to take maternity leave. Soon after, another school counselor resigned. The remaining school counselor is stomped with work as she is now nearly supporting 500 students. Which of the following is the best approach for the school counselor to do during this situation to best support the school?

    A. hire an administrative assistant that can support some minor issues
    B. focus on major issues that surface
    C. push some students to the assistant principal
    D. do not focus on the other two counselors workload

Answer: B

Explanation: With one school counselor, the best approach is to focus on major issues that surface. Minor issues can be deferred for later when additional school counselors are on site. Option A is not the best approach as the individual needs to be qualified. Option B and D do not support the school in a positive manner.

QUESTION 63

When establishing school counseling programs, which of the following is the most critical to consider for the school counselor?

    A. ensuring that the program has a long term vision
    B. identifying program belief that address how all students benefit
    C. ensuring that resources are available to provide appropriate support
    D. getting all staff, parents, and students aligned to the school counseling programs

Answer: B

Explanation: All options are to be considered, but the question asks for the "most critical." Option B is regarding how "all students benefit," which is most critical to consider when developing a school counseling programs.

QUESTION 64

Which of the following stages defines sexual maturity based on Sigmund Freud's theory of psychosexual development?

- A. phallic
- B. genital
- C. anal
- D. latency

Answer: B

Explanation: Sigmund Freud researched as a child and even as a teenager, individuals go through a series of stages in which growth and maturity occurs. Genital stage occurs typically in adolescence, in which people reach sexual maturity.

QUESTION 65

In which of the following situation is a certified counselor not required in school institutions?

- A. a school with little population
- B. an early childhood school
- C. a newly built public school
- D. a private school

Answer: D

Explanation: Private schools are not mandated by state/federal laws to have school counselor.

QUESTION 66

I. cognitive
II. behavior
III. affective

Of the above, which of the following do school counselors have impact on?

A. I only
B. I and II
C. II and III
D. I, II, and III

Answer: D

Explanation: School counselors have impact not only on cognitive or learning but also on important behavioral and affective measures.

QUESTION 67

A school counselor notices that a student's math standardize test scores are nearly perfect for several consecutive years. However, classroom grades on assignments and report card are below average or at average. Which of the following is the best first step to take to better understand the reasoning for the gap?

A. talk to the math teacher to get the math teacher's perspective on the gap
B. observe how the math teacher is providing instruction to the student
C. question the student regarding the gap and how the counselor can help
D. confirm that the student is not cheating on standardize tests

Answer: A

Explanation: The question asks for the first step to undertake, and the first step is to talk to the math teacher to get the math teacher's perspective on the gap. Observing the teacher instruct can be done after discussing with the teacher. Option C is also an approach to take, but that is not the first approach. Nothing in the question suggest the student cheated, so Option D is eliminated.

QUESTION 68

Which of the following is NOT considered a self-management skill?

- A. demonstrate ability to overcome barriers to learning
- B. demonstrate perseverance to achieve long- and short-term goals
- C. demonstrate critical-thinking skills to make informed decisions
- D. demonstrate ability to assume responsibility

Answer: C

Explanation: Demonstrate critical-thinking skills to make informed decisions is a learning strategy under the behavior standards under the American School Counselors Association Mindsets & Behaviors for Student Success.

QUESTION 69

In a session with a school counselor, a student provides very slight indication that the student might be having an inappropriate relationship with a teacher. What is the best action for the school counselor to take?

- A. move to another topic
- B. ignore the comment by the student
- C. ask more questions to get better understanding
- D. report the conversation to the school principal

Answer: C

Explanation: The student has provided a very slight indication that the student might be having an inappropriate relationship with a teacher. The school counselor does not have enough information to take any action, so the best approach is for the counselor to ask more questions to gain more information. From there, the counselor can decide what approach to take.

QUESTION 70

Steps to Program Development

8. Planning
9. Building the Foundation
10. Designing the Delivery System
11. Setting up the School Counseling Program
12. Working the School Counseling Program
13. Promoting the School Counseling Program
14. ?

Which of the follow completes the table above regarding steps to developing school counseling program?

A. Engaging teachers in participating
B. Monitoring program results
C. Ensuring all students benefit
D. Delivering the program

Answer: B

Explanation: After planning, designing, working, and promoting, the next step is going to be to monitor program results. As a school counselor, the need to know that the program is working is going to be done through monitoring the results.

QUESTION 71

Which of the following is the best for a school counselor to do to support English teachers in developing a lesson that delivers the guidance curriculum related to peer pressure?

- A. develop a slide pack on key aspects of peer pressure and the objectives of the guidance curriculum related to peer pressure
- B. conduct a training session with all teachers on peer pressure
- C. give teachers videos related to peer pressuring to use during the lesson
- D. provide assessment tools on guidance curriculum related to peer pressure to ensure students' learning

Answer: A

Explanation: The school counselor's goal is to ensure that the goals and objectives of the guidance curriculum related to peer pressure are being satisfied, so the best aspect is Option A.

QUESTION 72

A student has informed the school counselor that he will not be applying to colleges as his father got deported. The student does not see a point in getting further education as he will have to support his family. What can the school counselor do to assist the student?

- A. talk to the student about work and school life balance
- B. get the student connected with a immigration attorney
- C. discuss the long term benefits of a college education for his family
- D. talk about financial aid options available

Answer: C

Explanation: The student is not going to college because he wants to help his family. The best approach for the counselor to take is communicating the long term benefits of college for his family. That directly touches on his desires, and that can perhaps convince him to consider college.

QUESTION 73

A school counselor is providing students support in career exploration, and teaching respect for self and others. Which grade level is the school counselor supporting?

- A. second grade
- B. fifth grade
- C. seventh grade
- D. eleventh grade

Answer: C

Explanation: The keywords were "career exploration," which is appropriate for middle school students. Career awareness is appropriate for elementary education students. Career planning is focused for high school students.

QUESTION 74

Which of the following best describes situation where school counselor can break confidentiality?

- A. a student has cheated on homework assignment
- B. other students are at harm
- C. refusing to comply to punishment
- D. student is thinking about running away

Answer: B

Explanation: Under the law, school counselor can break confidentiality if students, teachers, or staff members are at risk of getting hurt.

QUESTION 75

According to John Holland's Theory of Vocational, which term describes students who are thinking rather than acting, and organizing and understanding rather than dominating or persuading?

- A. realistic
- B. social
- C. investigative
- D. enterprising

Answer: C

Explanation: According to John Holland's Theory of Vocational, there are six types: realistic, investigative, artistic, social, enterprising, and conventional. Investigative main characteristics include thinking rather than acting, and organizing and understanding rather than dominating or persuading.

QUESTION 76

Juan, a 19-year old high school senior, tells the school counselor that he plans to marry his 18-year-old girlfriend after graduation. Legally, the school counselor is required to

- A. call the parents of both students to inform them of the situation.
- B. inform the students they can't get married.
- C. do nothing since the students are of legal age to get married.
- D. do an exploration session with the two students to determine if marrying is the best option.

Answer: C

Explanation: The question ask what the school counselor should do under the law, and the school counselor is required to do nothing since the students are of legal age to get married.

QUESTION 77

Below is a document that the school counselor uses to gather information about students to better support them.

Student Behavior Data Collection Form

STUDENT_____**TEACHER**_____**DATE**_____

Performance Indicators: (+)=Excellent, (I)=Satisfactory, (-)=Area of Concern

Teacher Concerns (mark with X)	Observed Behaviors	Teacher Rating				
		Marking Period 1	Marking Period 2	Marking Period 3	Marking Period 4	Marking Period 5
	Section 1: Personal Development					
	Cooperates with others					
	Shows respect for others					
	Allows others to work undisturbed					
	Accepts responsibility for own misbehavior (e.g., provoking fights, bullying, fighting, defiant, anger, stealing)					
	Emotional Issues (e.g., perfectionism, anxiety anger, depression, suicide, aggression, withdrawn, low self-esteem)					
	Section 2: Career Development					
	Awareness of the World of Work					
	Self-Appraisal					
	Decision Making					
	Goal Setting					
	Section 3: Add Other Concerns:					
	External Issues (e.g., divorce, death, abuse, socio-economic, incarceration, military deployment)					
	Other					
	Section 4: School Record Data					
	Attendance: # of days absent					
	Attendance: # of days tardy					
	Discipline: # of referrals					
	Grades					
	School nurse visits					
	Test Scores					

In the above Student Behavior Data Collection Form, which of the following mistakes must be corrected?

- A. Change performance indicators to a number system instead of excellent, satisfactory, and area of concern.
- B. Teacher Rating needs to be changed to School Counselor Rating.
- C. Remove the Marking Period 5 as four periods is sufficient.
- D. Remove teacher concern column.

Answer: B

Explanation: This document is used primarily by the school counselor. There is a column for teachers to provide feedback on areas of concern. So, where it states Teacher Rating, that needs to be changed to School Counselor Rating.

QUESTION 78

In the observed behavior column, which of the following sections needs to be included to get a full picture of the students?

- A. Family Development
- B. Academic Development
- C. Social Development
- D. Peer Interaction

Answer: B

Explanation: The school counselor will need to have information regarding academic development, such as following directions, listening, staying on tasks, completing assignments, following rules, etc.

QUESTION 79

I. flexibility
II. willingness to listen
III. empathy

School counselors are advocates. Of the above, which of the following are characteristics that describe being an advocate?

A. I only
B. I and II
C. II and III
D. I, II, and III

Answer: D

Explanation: All options are characteristics that describe being an advocate for school counselors.

QUESTION 80

A school counselor is supporting a student that is feeling inferior. The school counselor encourages the student to be well aware of her surrounding and environment. As time goes by, the student learns to grapple her conscious levels of thought and is responsible for taking charge of changing behaviors. This situation best showed which of the following counseling theories?

A. The Gestalt Approach
B. The Person-Centered Approach
C. The Individual Psychology Approach
D. The Behavioral Approach

Answer: C

Explanation: This is a clear example of Individual Psychology Approach which is a theory of human behavior emphasizing the drive to overcome feelings of inferiority by compensation and the need to achieve personal goals.

QUESTION 81

A recent school survey showed that ninth grade female students are not interested in math and science subjects. In addition, recent assessment shows that male students are doing a lot better in math and science courses. The school counselor is looking to encourage more female students to become interested in math and science. Which of the following would be the best strategy to achieve this goal?

- A. assign math and science electives for female students
- B. start tutoring and mentoring program to increase female confidence in math and science
- C. have a group session with females to understand why they don't like math and science subjects
- D. encourage female students who are performing well to take more math and science courses

Answer: B

Explanation: The question states that female students are not interested and performing low relative to male students. Option B addresses both issues. Tutoring will help the female students to increase scores and mentoring can get them interested in math and science subjects.

QUESTION 82

I. facilitate the development of a plan of action
II. encourage the student to be more independent
III. be accessible to facilitate understanding between all involved parties (family, student, the future place of higher education).

Jimmy is starting his senior year at Roger High School. Since elementary school, he has had an IEP. As he has progressed in the educational system, his needs have changed as well. Jimmy is more concerned about his disability as he prepares for college. He and his parents have scheduled an appointment to speak with the school counselor. Of the above, which of the following is/are appropriate for the school counselor?

A. II only
B. III only
C. I and III
D. I, II and III

Answer: C

Explanation: The school counselor can assist in developing a transition plan along with being accessible to facilitate understanding between all involved parties for future education. There is no need for the school counselor to suggest that he needs to be independent due to his disability.

QUESTION 83

Which of the following is an indirect measure of achievement?

A. test results
B. retention rates
C. gifted screening
D. rank in class

Answer: C

Explanation: Indirect measures provide a less concrete view of student learning; for example, attitudes, perceptions, feelings, values, etc. Direct measures are those that measure student learning by assessing actual samples of student work. Option A, B, and D are relate to numbers, which are direct measure of achievement. Option C is an indirect measure of achievement.

QUESTION 84

Which of the following situations is best for the school counselor to use solution focused counseling?

A. an elementary student bullying classmates
B. a student worried about what career path to take
C. a student missing class three days of the week
D. a student with ADHD who is unwilling to complete assignments

Answer: B

Explanation: Solution focused counseling is focused more on solution-building rather than problem-solving. There is an acknowledgement of problems and past causes. However, this approach predominantly explores an individual's current resources and future hopes – helping them to look forward and use their own strengths to achieve their goals.

QUESTION 85

A high school counselor is working with a local college on implementing character education program. The local college professor has asked the school counselor to participate in a study to assess the impact of the character education classroom guidance program on the behavior of 10 children. For the study, the disciplinary records of these students will be used to complete the data. The school counselor has agreed to participate. Why is the school counselor agreeing to participate concerning?

A. the counselor did not ask the principal for permission
B. the counselor did not ask the parents for permission
C. the counselor might be violating FERPA laws
D. the counselor did nothing that is concerning

Answer: C

Explanation: Sharing students' data to third party is a violation of FERPA laws as the federal law protects the privacy of student educational records.

QUESTION 86

I. clarify ground rules and guidelines
II. discuss how to take notes
III. discuss confidentiality
IV. discuss active listening for each other

To ensure effective group counseling, in the first session, the high school counselor must discuss which of the following from above?

A. I and II
B. II and III
C. I, III, and IV
D. I, II, III, and IV

Answer: C

Explanation: The keywords in the question are "effective," "must," and "first session." Since this is the first session, establishing ground rules and guidelines will ensure stability and organization in the sessions. Confidentiality is critical in group counseling along with being active listeners.

QUESTION 87

A school counselor can provide professional counseling services to students referred by:

A. teachers
B. peers
C. nurse
D. all of the above

Answer: D

Explanation: School counselors can provide professional counseling services if referred by self, parents, teachers, administrators, school nurse, peers, outside agency, and others.

QUESTION 88

The Accountability Process

Step	Description
1	Mission - Connect the design and implementation of the school counseling program to the mission of the school.
2	Elements - Identify and examine the critical elements of the available data that are important to the school's mission.
3	Analyze - Analyze the critical data elements to see what they reveal, to identify problem areas, to establish baselines, and to set objectives.
4	Stakeholders-Unite – Identify stakeholders to be involved in addressing the movement of the critical data elements.
5	?
6	Educate – Inform all stakeholders of the changes in the targeted data elements that show the positive impact the school counseling program is having on student success.

Which of the following is the best description for Step 5?

A. Review – Reanalyze to determine whether the targeted results were satisfied.
B. Confirm – Rerun the program analysis to ensure the results are accurate.
C. Results – Reanalyze to determine whether the targeted results were satisfied.
D. Replicate – Rerun the program analysis to ensure the results are accurate.

Answer: C

Explanation: The fifth step is to reanalyze to determine whether the targeted results were satisfied, which is best labeled as Results.

QUESTION 89

Which of the following is NOT one of the major components of a comprehensive counseling and guidance program?

    A. Guidance Curriculum
    B. Individual Planning
    C. Responsive Services
    D. Monitoring Progress

Answer: D

Explanation: The four major components of a comprehensive counseling and guidance program are Guidance Curriculum, Individual Planning, Responsive Services, and System Support.

QUESTION 90

Which of the following best describes how might a student's test score be affected by a recent death in the family?

    A. remain the same
    B. marginally increase
    C. decrease substantially
    D. reduce to average scores

Answer: C

Explanation: When a student faces a death, he or she might miss several days of school or might not concentrate during class. This will have an impact on scores. The best description of what might happen to the score is decrease substantially.

QUESTION 91

According to Erik Erikson's theory of human development, individuals gain a sense of competency and accomplishment between the ages of _____.

A. 3 and 5
B. 6 and 12
C. 13 and 15
D. 15 and 18

Answer: B

Explanation: Erik Erikson saw psychosocial development as a sequence of stages, each described by specific goals, concerns, and accomplishments. According to Erik Erikson's theory of human development, individuals gain a sense of competency and accomplishment between the ages of 6 and 12. Between the ages of 6 and 12, the major psychosocial task is to solve the conflict between industry versus inferiority.

QUESTION 92

_____ give empirical data that allow goals and objectives to be established for a comprehensive guidance program.

A. Base assessments
B. Needs assessment
C. Informal assessments
D. Portfolios

Answer: B

Explanation: The main value of needs assessment is providing the counselor with empirical data that allow goals and objectives to be established for a comprehensive guidance program.

QUESTION 93

A school counselor has been informed that there are approximately 150 students without lockers due to availability. The school counselor will need to make a decision as to what action to take. Which of the following data is less likely needed to make an informed decision?

A. total number of lockers
B. total number of students
C. total number of broken lockers
D. total number of occupied lockers

Answer: D

Explanation: The school counselor will need the total number of lockers and number of students to confirm the problem does exist. As a school counselor, confirming a serious issue is important. Having the data on the total number of broken lockers will allow the school counselor to know if the issue is regarding over population of students or simply a locker availability/maintenance issue. Whether students are using the locker is not that relevant as all students will need a locker. Selecting some students to have lockers might result in discriminatory claims.

Using the following data to answer the next two questions.

Elementary Education – Grade 6

Summary of Student Performance for Core Subject Areas

- Reading Scores:
    - 85% of the students are performing below average
    - 65% of the struggling students are English Language Learners
    - 5% of the students are performing above average
- Math Scores
    - 87% of the students are performing below average
    - 5% of the struggling students are English Language Learners
    - 7% of the students are performing above average
- Writing Scores
    - 90% of the students are performing below average
    - 75% of the struggling students are English Language Learners
    - 6% of the students are performing above average

QUESTION 94

Which of the following is NOT supported by the data?

A. English Language Learners are doing better in reading than writing.
B. English Language Learners need help in reading and writing.
C. Non-English Language Learners need help mostly in math.
D. All students need help in at least one subject area.

Answer: D

Explanation: The data provided does not indicate that all students need help in at least one subject areas. In each area, there is a percent of students that are performing above average. It is possible the same student(s) are performing well in reading, writing, and math. All other options are supported by the data provided.

QUESTION 95

I. discussing with teacher on better supporting several students
II. counseling in a small-group afterschool
III. helping students develop personal goals

Of the above, which of the following is/are direct student services that a school counselor can provide?

A. I only
B. I and II
C. II and III
D. I, II, and III

Answer: C

Explanation: The school counselor discussing with a teacher on better supporting students is an indirect student service. The students are not in direct interaction with the school counselor. Counseling in a small-group afterschool and helping students develop personal goals are direct student services as students are directly involved with the school counselor.

QUESTION 96

Which of the following is the greatest need for improvement based on the data?

A. improvement in writing for nearly all students
B. improvement in reading for English Language Learners
C. improvement in grammar for nearly all students
D. improvement in math for non-English Language Learners

Answer: A

Explanation: The data shows the sixth-grade class is not doing well in most areas. The greatest area of improvement needed is in writing scores as nearly 90% of the students are below average. Option C does not directly support the data. Option B and C are areas of improvement but not the greatest areas requiring improvement.

QUESTION 97

Goal of Elementary Education:
Ensuring all students has equitable access to learning curriculum.

The school counselor is seeking to determine how well this goal is being achieved. Which of the following approaches would be the best to implement?

A. visiting classrooms while teachers are instructing
B. analyzing culture background of students who have improved
C. reviewing disaggregated results from several recent assessments
D. discussing with students about recent lessons instructed by the teacher

Answer: C

Explanation: The school counselor will have a better understanding if the goal is being achieved by reviewing data separated into components of recent assessments.

QUESTION 98

The school counselor has noticed a school trend toward declining math scores on statewide assessments. The school counselor desires to plan professional development activities to address the problem. Which of the following is the best first action to take during the planning process?

- A. interview teachers to see what methods are currently being used
- B. organize a team of teachers to come up with professional development activities
- C. analyze test results to understand specific math skills requiring improvement and subgroups of students requiring additional support
- D. analyze test results of previous years with excellent performance on statewide assessments and understand the methods used during instruction at the time

Answer: C

Explanation: To develop the professional development activities, the school counselor first needs to understand the specifics of the problem. The best approach is to review the data to see which skills the students (or subgroups of students) need most help with. This will set the foundation to developing effective professional development activities.

QUESTION 99

The Family Educational Rights and Privacy Act of 1974 give parents/guardians of a minor who is getting special needs services the right to

- A. remove their child from standardize exams.
- B. obtain educational records to share with non-school individuals.
- C. select special education services.
- D. opt out of IEP meetings.

Answer: B

Explanation: The Family Educational Rights and Privacy Act of 1974 give parents or guardians of a minor to obtain copies of students' academic records to share with individuals outside of the school system.

QUESTION 100

Which of the following is a type of test score that indicates a student's relative position among a group of students in the same grade who are tested at the same time?

A. raw score
B. average score
C. percentile rank
D. composite score

Answer: C

Explanation: A student's percentile rank indicates the percent of students in a particular group that received raw scores lower than the raw score of the student. It shows the student's relative position among a group of students.

QUESTION 101

A description of the student's current academic achievement level and functional performance is required by:

A. Daily Assessment Records
B. IEP
C. IFSP
D. 504 Plan

Answer: B

Explanation: Individualized Education Program (IEP) requires a description of the student's current academic achievement level and functional performance.

QUESTION 102

A school counselor has notice that too many elementary education students at a K-6th grade-level school are bringing cell phones to school. Which of the following is the best and appropriate approach to resolve the problem?

- A. have metal dictators daily when students enter the school
- B. not to return confiscated cell phones back to students or parents
- C. implement a harsher punishment for students who bring cell phones
- D. send a letter to inform parents of cell phone policy and have parents sign the letter

Answer: D

Explanation: The keywords in the question are "best" and "appropriate." For elementary students to have cell phones means those parents are allowing them to have those items. Parents need to be re-informed about the policy to not allow their children come with cell phones to schools. Having the parents sign the letter shows they have read the policy. Option A is a good idea, but it is not appropriate for elementary students.

QUESTION 103

A school counselor has notice that certain eighth-grade students, such as ELLs and students with an economically disadvantaged classification, tend to perform much lower than their peers on assignments. Which of the following professional development activity is the best for the teachers to undertake to support struggling students?

- A. establishing assessments that are tailored to struggling students
- B. providing differentiated instruction that builds on students' strength
- C. reviewing instructional methods that have worked with some students
- D. understanding different ways of learning in different countries and cultures

Answer: B

Explanation: Students who are ELL or economically disadvantaged have different ways of learning. In fact, all students learn differently. Having the knowledge to differentiate instruction that builds on students' strength will support in providing better instruction, allowing possible improvement on assignments.

QUESTION 104

A school surveys students about their interests in subject areas; the students' responses matter because they are?

- A. relevant
- B. valid
- C. measurable
- D. consistent

Answer: A

Explanation: The students can fill the survey out randomly without any interest, so the responses are not always valid or consistent. There is no indication that the responses are measurable. The students' interest is relevant to learning.

QUESTION 105

Strengthening instructional decision making is best done by which with of the following?

- A. having access to wide range data on students' assessment for different grade levels
- B. having understanding of students' background information
- C. having access to updated worksheets and lesson plans
- D. having understanding of current standards

Answer: A

Explanation: The keyword in the question is "best." Option A and B seem like possible answers, but Option A is correct as the assessment data will give more knowledge of students' abilities. This is more powerful in instructional decision making than understanding of students' background information.

QUESTION 106

A school counselor, a principal, and grade level teachers are getting together to discuss math scores to improve scores for the following school year. What kind of meeting are they holding?

A. school improvement planning
B. grade level planning
C. teacher development planning
D. district improvement planning

Answer: A

Explanation: The school counselor, principal, and grade level teachers are looking to improve scores for the next school year, so they are involved in a school improvement planning.

QUESTION 107

A school counselor is approached by a parent who is displeased about instruction relating to world religions that is included in history class. Which of the following described by the parent should be the most concerning to the school counselor?

A. questioning the existence of God
B. promoting one religion to be more worthy than another
C. having students to learn about practices of different religions
D. allowing students to share information about their own religion

Answer: B

Explanation: The teacher can teach religion in history course; however, the teacher cannot promote one religion to be more worthy than another. Option C is not as concerning as the answer choice states "learn," which is acceptable in history courses.

QUESTION 108

Which of the following is strictly considered morally unethical?

A. School counselor is taking money from the school operating budget to buy personal items.
B. School counselor using staff time to create worksheets to market online for personal gain.
C. School counselor refusing to provide information to parents regarding his child's grades.
D. School counselor seeking donations for school events from local businesses.

Answer: B

Explanation: The keywords in the question are "strictly" and "morally unethical." Option A is considered illegal. Option B is morally unethical as the teacher should not be using staff time for personal gain. Option C is not the best approach for school counselor to take, but it is not morally unethical. There is nothing morally unethical about seeking donations for school events from local businesses.

QUESTION 109

At a high school, the graduation rate is very high, but the number of students applying to college is 50% of the graduating rate. Which of the following is the best way to increase college admission?

A. educate the students about opportunities associated with obtaining a college education
B. give students fee waivers, so they don't have to pay for college application fee
C. support students in preparation for SAT and ACT exams
D. provide students with support in applying for colleges

Answer: D

Explanation: The issue is concerning that many students are not applying to college. With a high graduation rate, the students demonstrate the ability to further education. The way to support students is to provide assistance in applying for colleges as the process can be long and confusing to some individuals.

QUESTION 110

Which of the following is the best type of assessment to provide useful feedback for professional development?

- A. circular assessment
- B. formative assessment
- C. summative assessment
- D. quantitative assessment

Answer: B

Explanation: Formative assessment is ongoing throughout the year for the purpose of improving performance. This is the best way to provide constant feedback for development.

QUESTION 111

- I. evaluating data to make decision on achieving vision and goals
- II. aligning all resources, including technology to achieve the vision
- III. outlining criteria to show how instructional programs support the vision

Which of the following are needed to ensure continuous improvement toward the vision and goals of schools?

- A. I and II
- B. I and III
- C. II and III
- D. I, II, and III

Answer: D

Explanation: To ensure continuous improvement toward the vision and goals of schools, school counselors must evaluate data, align resources, and outline criteria to support the vision and goals.

QUESTION 112

The Individuals with Disabilities Education Improvement Act (IDEA)

  A. forces federal government to provide federal funding for early childhood programs.
  B. requires states to create early intervention programs.
  C. requires schools to have funding for improving technology for early childhood special education students.
  D. requires states to provide data to the federal government on student progress in core academic areas.

Answer: B

Explanation: The Act does not force federal government to give funding, require schools to have funding for technology, or require states to provide data. The Act does require states to create early intervention programs.

QUESTION 113

In decision making process concerning curriculum, the group that is not needed is _____.

  A. curriculum experts
  B. professional staff
  C. school counselors
  D. parents

Answer: D

Explanation: Recommended practice suggest that parents are not involved in decision making process concerning curriculum.

QUESTION 114

Which of the following is the primary purpose of scaffolding student learning?

- A. ensure students' learning
- B. assist students to become independent learners
- C. encourage positive group engagement
- D. assist students in independently completing assessment

Answer: B

Explanation: The purpose of scaffolding is to get students knowledgeable to allow them to independently complete activities.

QUESTION 115

An open school event is being held at an elementary school. Which of the following is the most effective strategy for showing respect to and sensitivity to the cultural diversity among the families?

- A. have staff to translate for necessary families
- B. have written communication in multiple languages
- C. have staff to support students with disabilities
- D. have student-made posters of different cultures around the school

Answer: A

Explanation: Having staff members translate for families with home languages other than English is the most effective strategy. This shows that the school took extra steps to ensure that information is communicated and questions are being asked by all individuals.

QUESTION 116

Which of the following is the best way for a school counselor to reduce his or her workload?

- A. add more support staff
- B. delegate responsibilities
- C. work during lunch hour
- D. focus on major issues

Answer: B

Explanation: In organizations, delegating responsibilities is an approach to decreasing workload. In school organization, this can also promote development of leadership skills. Adding more staff can reduce workload, but there is a cost associated with this approach. Option A is not the best answer.

QUESTION 117

What is the maximum number of days a special education student can be suspended?

- A. 3 days
- B. 5 days
- C. 10 days
- D. 15 days

Answer: C

Explanation: After 10 school days, under IDEA, students with disabilities must get educational services.

QUESTION 118

Which of the following is needed to make an informed decision regarding school dilemmas?

- A. data
- B. support
- C. options
- D. alternatives

Answer: A

Explanation: The keywords in the question are "informed decision." In order to make decisions, it is critical to have data. Data can be analyzed to know the positives and negatives and allow an informed decision.

QUESTION 119

A school counselor is very unhappy with a new district policy. The school counselor has expressed her concern to the district, but the district stands by the policy. The school counselor should

- A. ignore the policy.
- B. follow the policy.
- C. get parents to express concern.
- D. continue to contest the policy.

Answer: B

Explanation: School counselors will not always like the policies that are implemented. Regardless, polices need to be followed. Option B is the best answer.

QUESTION 120

The school counselor is reaching out to members of various demographic groups that make up the school community to support in playing an active role in the school. The school counselor's action best demonstrates

- A. gaining support for success.
- B. getting different ideas to ensure success.
- C. supporting school success by valuing diversity.
- D. ensuring that the community is involved in school decision making process.

Answer: C

Explanation: The question states "various demographic groups." The school counselor is valuing diversity to ensure success of the school.

QUESTION 121

For the school year, the district has adopted new standards, and students are going to be tested on those standards for the upcoming statewide assessments. Towards the end of the school year, more and more parents are opting their child out of the assessment. In this situation, what is the most appropriate action for the school counselor to undertake?

- A. inform parents that students have been exposed to these standards for some time and the school has prepared the students
- B. inform parents that standards are going to be updated to meet the needs of the future
- C. deny the parents request to opt students out of the assessment
- D. convey the benefits of the assessments to the parents

Answer: A

Explanation: Informing parents that the students are prepared for the updated standards will give confidence to the parents the students are ready. Option A is the most appropriate to communicate.

QUESTION 122

Which of the following is the most important question to answer when using community resources for school purposes?

- A. Are there enough resources to impact the entire school?
- B. Do the resources meet the needs of the school?
- C. Have these resources been used in the past?
- D. What are the limitations of the resources?

Answer: B

Explanation: If the resources do not meet the needs of the school, there is no need to pursue in using the resources.

QUESTION 123

The school counselor has notice that there are many English Language Learners (ELL) at the school. In reviewing the students' records, most of the students have been classified as ELL for over 5 years. Why is this concerning?

- A. The school does not have assessment tools to determine if ELL learners are ready to go into regular classrooms.
- B. There is nothing concerning about students being classified as ELL for over 5 years.
- C. The school will need more ELL teachers, which might be difficult to recruit.
- D. The students are not being taught effectively to come out of ELL classrooms.

Answer: D

Explanation: The goal is to eventually have ELL students enter into regular classroom. For students to be classified as ELL for over 5 years indicates there is something wrong with instructional methods. There is nothing to suggest assessment tools are lacking as the school counselor is reviewing records.

QUESTION 124

    I.   Cognitive behavioral play therapy involves child in counseling play.

    II.   Cognitive behavioral play therapy is open ended.

    III.   Cognitive behavioral play therapy allows development of adaptive thoughts and behaviors.

Cognitive behavioral play therapy places a very strong emphasis on the student's involvement in the process of developing appropriate social skills. Of the above, which of the following are properties of cognitive behavioral play therapy?

    A. I and II
    B. I and III
    C. II and III
    D. I, II, and III

Answer: B

Explanation: Cognitive behavioral play therapy is structured, directive, and goal-oriented, rather than open ended.

QUESTION 125

To improve organization within the school system, the most important factor in sampling public opinion about education is:

A. population size
B. sample size
C. random size
D. representativeness of sample

Answer: D

Explanation: To improve organization within the school system, having a good representativeness of sample is critical. A representative sample is a small quantity of something that accurately reflects the larger entity.

QUESTION 126

A middle school is seeking to start a program by getting talented, skilled community members to communicate the importance of learning or to speak at assemblies. To ensure the program is the best, which of the following factor should be given the highest priority?

A. the number of years of experience the individuals have in their field of expertise
B. the number of awards the individuals have in their field of expertise
C. the relevance of the individuals' experience to the school curriculum
D. the relevance of the individuals having a degree related to their job

Answer: C

Explanation: When doing a program, the school needs to ensure that the program is aligned to the school curriculum. Having a program aligned to school curriculum will further students' learning.

QUESTION 127

Which of the following is the most important issue to correct when it comes to the school safety and security?

- A. multiple entrances that are unmonitored
- B. metal detectors that were installed years ago
- C. emergency procedures reviewed over 5 years ago
- D. new teachers not trained for emergency response

Answer: A

Explanation: Entrances need to be monitored either by people or cameras. This is the most important issue to correct when it comes to the school safety and security of the options provided.

QUESTION 128

Which of the following will receive the greatest consideration in establishing comprehensive program for student activities in schools?

- A. needs of the facilities
- B. input from school staff
- C. the staffing requirements
- D. developmental needs of the students

Answer: C

Explanation: The question asks for the "greatest consideration." When planning programs for students, resources are needed, so staffing requirements will be the greatest consideration taken into account.

QUESTION 129

A school counselor will be engaging staff member to select activities for the upcoming school year for parents and students to participate. Which of the following is the most important question to consider to ensure effective decision making?

- A. Will the activities allow all the students and parents to participate?
- B. What resources will be required for the activities?
- C. Will the activities be within the defined budget?
- D. Will the activities reflect the school goals?

Answer: D

Explanation: The keyword in the question is "most." When developing activities, the school counselor needs to ensure that the activities are aligned to the goals. If there are aligned to the goals, the activities will further learning of students. Other options are questions to consider but not the most important.

QUESTION 130

One of the middle school students in Mr. Matt science class stated "Why can't I just pay you to give me good grades like Mr. Bark in math class?" The science teacher informs the school counselor of what was said by the student. Which of the following is the best action for the school counselor to take?

- A. tell the teacher to inform the principal
- B. talk to the student who made the statement
- C. review grades given by the math teacher to see irregularities
- D. nothing as this is just a student making a statement with no proof

Answer: A

Explanation: The best action for the school counselor to take is informing the teacher to inform the principal. If the school counselor informs the principal, that is secondhand information being communicated. The teacher learned of the information first, so the teacher needs to communicate it to the principal. From there, the principal can review the grades given by the math teacher to see irregularities. If there are obvious irregularities, the principal can discuss with the math teacher.

QUESTION 131

  I.   Access by minors to inappropriate matter on the Internet and World Wide Web
  II. The safety and security of minors when using electronic mail, chat rooms, and other forms of direct electronic communications
  III. Unauthorized access including "hacking" and other unlawful activities by minors online
  IV. Unauthorized disclosure, use, and dissemination of personal information regarding minors

Of the above, which of the following are addressed by the Children's Internet Protection Act (CIPA)?

  A. I only
  B. I and II
  C. II, and III
  D. I, II, III, and IV

Answer: D

Explanation: All the above are addressed in the Children's Internet Protection Act.

QUESTION 132

  I.   suspend the boy for five days
  II. conduct a meeting with the boy's parents
  III. have the boy complete bullying prevention training with the school counselor

A seventh girl has informed the school counselor that a boy in her class has been verbally bullying her for the past month. The boy has said that the girl is fat, smelly, and ugly. The boy has confessed to this. Which of the following is/are the action(s) to take?

  A. I only
  B. I and II
  C. I and III
  D. II and III

Answer: D

Explanation: The action to take is conduct a meeting with the boy's parents to communicate this type of behavior is unacceptable. Bullying is a serious issue and needs to be addressed, so the boy needs to complete bullying prevention training with the school counselor.

QUESTION 133

Having a strong school organization requires a good decision-making process. For school counselors the decision making process involves all the following except?

- A. understanding the problem
- B. considering views of opposing staff
- C. remaining firm with decisions
- D. having a unbiased mindset

Answer: C

Explanation: Good decision making process involves understanding the problem, considering views of opposing staff, and having a unbiased mindset. With new information or other circumstances, decisions might need to be modified.

QUESTION 134

The goal of a group is to improve parents' involvement in students' learning and performance. The group has developed the plan and is in the process of implementing the plan to involve parents. Which of the following needs to be undertaken to ensure that the plan is effective?

- A. have parents complete a survey on the plan
- B. track the number of parents involved
- C. track students' performance
- D. ensure the objective of the plan is communicated

Answer: B

Explanation: A plan is developed to get more parents involved in students' learning. To know the plan is working data needs to be tracked on the number of parents that get involved. If few parents are getting involved, then the plan is ineffective. If a lot of parents are getting involved, the plan is effective.

QUESTION 135

Jenny is a school counselor at a local elementary school. One of her goals for the new school year is to ensure all individuals have an environment that shows commitment to the belief that all individuals can learn and succeed. Jenny can best support this vision across the school, by having teachers value which classroom practice?

   A. use various instructional method to support all students in classroom throughout the year
   B. provide monthly engagement to obtain input from students and teachers on what works and what does not work
   C. ensure that state standards are being following to ensure excellence in performance base testing
   D. having more interactive and fun educational activities and field trips

Answer: A

Explanation: The goal of the school is to ensure all students can learn and succeed, so the best way to do that is using various instructional methods to support all students in classroom. This approach has greater impact to all students.

QUESTION 136

Communication is vital part in ensuring robust school organization. Communication among group members is connected to which of the following?

   A. relationship
   B. trust
   C. organization
   D. conformity

Answer: B

Explanation: Trust and communication are linked together to ensure robust school organization. When trust is established, the information that is communicated is taken without doubt.

QUESTION 137

To ensure mission of school organization expectations are consistent, goals need to be all the following except:

A. clear
B. accepted
C. attainable
D. measurable

Answer: B

Explanation: Goals need to be clear to ensure understanding. Goals have to be attainable. Otherwise, individuals will lose interest. Goals must be measured to track achievement. Goals do not have to be accepted by everyone.

QUESTION 138

Which of the following types of behavior best shows a school counselor's sensitivity to the needs of an organization?

A. opening an anonymous survey for teacher
B. conducting engagement sessions with school staff
C. ensuring multiple family engagement with parents and staff
D. establishing two way communication with responding to needs

Answer: D

Explanation: Having a two way communication system and responding to needs are characteristics of school counselor's sensitivity to the needs of an organization.

QUESTION 139

Which of the following is the main purpose of involving students, parents, and teachers in the education decision-making process in schools?

- A. obtain various inputs from different groups
- B. prevent groups from dominating decisions
- C. ensure proper representation of individuals
- D. ensure involvement of all stakeholders

Answer: A

Explanation: Involving students, parents, and teachers in the education decision-making process in schools allows various different inputs to be obtained. This ensures that learning needs are addressed for a wider group and allows different ideas to be communicated.

QUESTION 140

Special education programs are populated with students from particular cultural background and language background. School counselors need to take which of the following approach to ensure proper identification of individuals entering the special education program?

- A. conduct interviews to confirm students need to be in the special education program
- B. have assessment tools that take into consideration that students are from different backgrounds from language and culture standpoint.
- C. use proper assessment processes with students prior to being identified as special education student
- D. review the placement procedures currently used to determine if the student grade level is correct

Answer: C

Explanation: Proper assessment processes are critical to ensure that the students need to be in special education programs. Option A is not effective. Option B is wrong as assessment tools do not need to take into consideration that students are from different backgrounds from language and culture standpoint. Option D is discussing grade level, which the question is not referring too. The best option is C.

QUESTION 141

The school counselor has abruptly decided to resign. The position is vacant and will take several weeks or perhaps a month to fill. What is the best action for the school to take?

A. ask the state to send a temporary school counselor
B. hold off on discussing students' issues until a replacement is found
C. review current staff to see who has the best qualification to temporary provide school counselor support
D. have the school physiologist fill the position of the school counselor

Answer: C

Explanation: The school counselor is a vital role in the school's organization. The best approach is to assign an individual with acceptable qualification to temporary provide school counselor support. Option A might be a good option, but having someone already in the school staff to support the activities is better as there is a less learning curve of how the school operates. Option B is not the best approach; issues need to be resolved. Option D is not the best approach as the qualifications of school counselor and school physiologist are different.

QUESTION 142

Which of the following is the least effective way for elementary students to learn content?

A. lecture
B. cooperative learning
C. direct instruction
D. modeling

Answer: A

Explanation: The least effective learning method for elementary students is lecturing as there is little interaction with the students.

QUESTION 143

   I. coming to school very irritable
   II. being hyperactive most of the day
   III. fighting with other children

The first step the school counselor needs to take in this situation is to:

A. refer the student to the school nurse for deficit/hyperactivity disorder symptoms
B. monitor the behavior for few months to discuss with the principal
C. discuss with parents on home behavior
D. develop an intervention plan to support the student

Answer: D

Explanation: The goal is to support the student to prevent the actions that are outlined. To do that, the best approach is to engage with the administrator and develop an intervention plan to support the student.

QUESTION 144

Blake is a new student from another state, and he has separation anxiety. At the beginning of class during circle time, he does not want to let his father go. The best action for the teacher is to:

A. have the father come visit Blake a couple of times per day
B. have the father remain with Blake for 15 minutes and, then, ask him to leave
C. have the father participate in circle time, and when Blake is involved, have the parent sneak out of the room
D. introduce Blake to two friends and ask him to sit between them and engage in a discussion

Answer: D

Explanation: Having the father come visit a couple of times per day is not normal practice, so A is not the correct answer. Choice B involves the father leaving abruptly, which will not support the student's separation anxiety. Choice C seems like a good option, but because it asks for the father to participate in the circle time, Choice C is not the best option. Introducing Blake to several friends and having him engage with them will distract Blake and allow the parent to leave.

QUESTION 145

Which statement would be classified as a long term goal rather than a course or lesson objective?

- A. The student will analyze independently informational text.
- B. The student will be able to identify the verbs in a paragraph.
- C. The student will be able to develop a well organized presentation.
- D. The student will be able to identify main ideas.

Answer: A

Explanation: Analyzing independently is a skill that will take some time to develop, so this is consider a long term goal.

QUESTION 146

A school counselor has been working at a school for three months. After evaluating the needs of the district, the school counselor has been informed that she will have to go to another school. The school counselor refuses this move, and she takes action to abandon the position without in advance notification. The school counselor has:

- A. inappropriately abandon the position
- B. the right to abandon the position
- C. taken appropriate action
- D. breached the contract

Answer: D

Explanation: The contracts of teachers indicate that an advanced notification is required prior to leaving the position. Moreover, common practice is to give an advanced notification, so the school can make arrangements for temporary or permanent replacement.

QUESTION 147

IDEA covers which of the following disabilities from birth:

      I.   cerebral palsy
      II.   visual impairment
      III. Down syndrome
      IV. hearing impairment

A. I and III
B. II and IV
C. I and II
D. III and IV

Answer: A

Explanation: Cerebral palsy and Down syndrome are conditions that cause severe learning disabilities and cognitive developmental issues. Cerebral palsy and Down syndrome are covered from birth under IDEA.

QUESTION 148

A school counselor overhears a student picking on another student. The student says "you look very ugly with glasses." What is the best phrase for the school counselor to say to the student doing the picking?

A. we treat all of our classmates with respect
B. we all look different, it's no need to point it out
C. we do not want to be mean to others
D. glasses are to help people see better

Answer: A

Explanation: Choice A gives the student doing the picking directions on how to interact with classmates in a respectful manner. Choice B is a fact, but not the best statement as it does not create an environment to respect others. Choice C is similar to Choice A, but Choice A is more positive. Choice D does not resolve the issue of the student picking on another student.

QUESTION 149

   I. parents
   II. regular education teacher(s)
   III. special education teacher(s)

According to IDEA 2004, an IEP team meeting consists of which of the following from above?

A. I and II
B. I and III
C. II and III
D. I, II, and III

Answer: D

Explanation: Parents, at least one regular education teacher, and at least one special education teacher are needed in an IEP meeting.

QUESTION 150

A four-year-old uses both English and Spanish languages at home. Discussing with the school counselor, the grandfather expressed concerns that his child sometimes mixes up words between the two languages. Which of the following would be the best response for the school counselor to provide the grandfather?

A. document instances of the child mixing words to see if patterns exist
B. inform the grandfather that this will continue for many years to come
C. inform grandfather that this is common for the child's age
D. conduct a formal assessment for placement of special education services

Answer: C

Explanation: Young children exposed to two languages at an early age typically mix up words between the two languages. The best approach is to inform the grandfather of this information to alleviate his concerns.

OAE 040 School Counselor

By: Preparing Teachers In America™